FINDING THE CONNECTIONS

FINDING THE CONNECTIONS

Linking Assessment, Instruction, and Curriculum in ELEMENTARY MATHEMATICS

JEAN MOON & LINDA SCHULMAN

HEINEMANN
Portsmouth, NH

Heinemann
A division of Reed Elsevier Inc.
361 Hanover Street   Portsmouth, NH 03801-3912
Offices and agents throughout the world

The authors and the publisher would like to thank the teachers, children, and parents who have given their permission to include material in this book. Every effort has been made to contact the copyright holders and the children and their parents for permission to reprint borrowed material. We regret any oversights that may have occurred and would be happy to rectify them in future printings of this work. We would like to thank the following for permission to include previously published material:

Figure 5.1 from A QUESTION OF THINKING: A FIRST LOOK AT STUDENTS' PERFORMANCE ON OPEN-ENDED QUESTIONS IN MATHEMATICS, California Assessment Program. Copyright © 1989. Reprinted by permission of the California State Department of Education.

Figure 5.8 from HOW TO EVALUATE PROGRESS IN PROBLEM SOLVING by Randall Charles and Frank Lester. Copyright © 1988. Reprinted by permission of the National Council of Teachers of Mathematics.

Figure 5.14 from MATHEMATICS ASSESSMENT: MYTHS, MODELS, GOOD QUESTIONS, AND PRACTICAL SUGGESTIONS, edited by Jean Kerr Stenmark. Copyright © 1991. Reprinted by permission of the National Council of Teachers of Mathematics.

Editor: Toby Gordon
Copy Editor: Alan Huisman
Production Editor: Renée M. Pinard
Text Designer: Jenny Jensen Greenleaf
Cover Designer: Darci Mehall

Library of Congress Cataloging-in-Publication Data
Moon, C. Jean.
    Finding the connections : linking assessment, instruction, and
curriculum in elementary mathematics / C. Jean Moon, Linda Schulman.
        p.   cm.
    Includes bibliographical references (p.   –   ).
    ISBN 0-435-08370-8 (acid-free)
    1. Mathematics—Study and teaching (Elementary)—Evaluation.
    2. Mathematical ability—Testing. I. Schulman, Linda. II. Title.
QA135.5.M6156   1995
372.7—dc20   94-46724
                                                    CIP

Printed in the United States of America on acid-free paper
99 98 97 96 95 EB 5 4 3 2 1

CONTENTS

PREFACE

The idea for any book comes from a configuration of many smaller ideas threaded together, at first not necessarily into a sense-making whole. Ideas grow and develop from observing and listening to others with similar thoughts and interests until, slowly, there is a sense of something larger than just an idea, a bigger story that should be shared.

And so it was with this book. We come from different academic backgrounds, professional experiences, even areas of the country. Jean's doctorate is in learning and development and evaluation. Her professional journey as an educator started at Alverno College in Milwaukee, Wisconsin, where she was director of the Assessment Center. Since that time Jean has applied her academic expertise to mathematics, science, and technology education in K–12 settings and has served as an evaluator of several nationally funded projects focused on teacher professional development. Currently, she is director of the Center for Mathematics, Science, and Technology in Education at Lesley College. Linda started her professional journey as a fourth-grade teacher in Massachusetts and now has a doctorate in mathematics education. For the past eighteen years she has been involved in mathematics and teacher training at Lesley College. Linda has coauthored numerous curriculum materials for teaching mathematics at the K–12 level, most of which focus on the development of problem-solving abilities.

Our varied backgrounds and experiences helped shape our ideas about many professional interests—teaching, learning, the professional development of teachers, and testing—before our collaboration at Lesley College. The energy for this book came as we shared ideas with each other about mathematics reform as well as alternative assessment and formed a commitment to communicate these ideas to others.

The field of alternative, authentic, or performance-based assessment (whichever term you prefer) is an emerging one, and the questions related to it are also evolving:

1. What performance indicators are appropriate benchmarks against which to describe student growth?
2. How can teachers make assessment a natural extension of their instruction?
3. How can teachers involve students more actively in the students' own learning?
4. How can teachers create assessment strategies that are rich in context and accessible to all students?

5. How can teachers build instructional lessons around the big ideas in mathematics?

No one person or group has all the answers, and perhaps that is the way it will be for some time to come.

There is a growing awareness of the place and power of alternative assessment as a process to inform teachers, students, and parents about student learning in all subject areas. We find it to be particularly true in mathematics. For years this country's testing traditions have valued correct answers and the ability to do repeated computational tasks over the acquisition of a developmental picture of a student's conceptual understanding considered essential to mathematical literacy. Equating the ability to produce right answers with understanding essential mathematical concepts is now being understood as somewhat off the mark. And that represents good news to the many, many teachers, administrators, and parents who for years have felt intuitively that what students learned was not always tapped by what was designated as a fair test. Those most uncomfortable with the status awarded multiple-choice tests and tests focusing on correct answers were aware that often more is learned from a student's explanation or justification of an answer than from the answer itself. From our perspective the real power of performance-based assessment rests in an ability to craft a process that provides realistic descriptions of student work, not just numerical answers.

This book provides practitioners with an introduction to alternative assessment that is comprehensive, practical, and, to the degree allowed by the printed page, interactive. We have tried to present the theoretical and practical aspects of assessment in a way that suggests the very process-oriented nature of alternative assessment rather than a fixed end point. Knowledge about assessment increases the more assessment is practiced. NCTM's *Professional Standards for Teaching Mathematics* and *Curriculum and Evaluation Standards for School Mathematics* suggest that children grow in mathematical literacy only if they "do" mathematics, and we believe the same is true of assessment. Teachers can grow in their ability to understand the richness of alternative assessment only if they "do" it and then share those experiences with colleagues and reflect on what they have done.

We also include student work whenever possible, since this too represents some of the "doing." Many teachers now use alternative assessment, and we feel the work of their students will enrich your thinking as it has our own.

As the title suggests, this book addresses the many connections found in alternative assessment: connections between assessment and curriculum, assessment and instruction, students and assessment, parents and assessment, schools and their communities, and teachers and their colleagues. The number of connections involved in the alternative assessment process adds to its complexity but also its richness.

Like most books, this one was written with the assistance of others. We want to acknowledge this assistance not only because we are so very grateful for it but because it models an important process—collaboration. For your help, your excitement about our work, and your willingness to share your professional expertise we thank you, Elizabeth Badger, Cheryl Chedester and the teachers in Kentucky, Kathy Cusson, Rebecca Eston, Judy McVarish, Jessica Rubin, the Exxon K–3 Math Specialist Project teachers from Garfield Elementary in Wisconsin, the teachers in Lesley's Summer Assessment Institutes, and all the K–3 teacher-leaders in Project BEST at Lesley College: Marilee Cantelmo, Kathy Carloni, Gail Connolly, Mary Daiopulos, David Downing, Lisa Durrell, Jeanine Freimont, Kathy Graf, Lee Hardaway, Mary Hill, Mary Jo Jones, Kathryn Judd, Vicky Kherlopian, Mary Marden, Rayma Mui, Beth Nasson, Liz Raycoft, Lisa Smart, Wendy Tompkins, Paula Tranchita, Susan Weiss, and Sharon Zagaria. You have helped us refine our own conceptual understandings of assessment, shared your work with us, and moved us forward with new questions.

We'd also like to thank our many students over the years with whom we have been able to experiment with alternative assessment in our own practices. And we would like to thank Toby Gordon and the many other talented people we encountered at Heinemann who have made this book a reality.

Finally, we need to recognize the people who sustain us through any writing project. For Jean they are Vicki and Douglas—for patience, for unending interest and support, for belief in the process, for terrific questions, for gifted editing skills, for reminding me of what is important while at the same time pushing me on, thank you. For Linda it is John—for once again providing a continuous supply of love, assurance, intelligence, encouragement, and support, thank you.

· 1 ·

Finding Our Way

*I have never taught math like this
before. It is so exciting. The children love
using manipulatives and I am getting
more comfortable with mathematics too.
I am ready, now, to think about
assessment. It feels like the next step.*

IN THIS CHAPTER

- Why do we need new assessment strategies?
- What is alternative assessment and what does it involve?
- How will alternative assessment strategies change my mathematics teaching?
- How can this book help me use new assessment strategies in my classroom?

KEY TERMS

Alternative assessment is just one of the names given to nontraditional methods of evaluating student learning. These different names are often used interchangeably, although each term emphasizes a different aspect of the general concept. Alternative assessment emphasizes that methods used to collect information about student learning are different from traditional paper-and-pencil tests, which are standardized and often appear in a multiple-choice format.

Assessment strategy refers to the way in which information about student learning is collected. Assesment strategies include interviews, observations, portfolios, projects, journals, open-ended questions, and self- and peer assessments.

Authentic assessment is another term used to refer to nontraditional assessment practices. The term emphasizes the fact that assessment tasks must authentically represent the way in which the learning has been conducted,

1

be worthwhile, represent the way in which the tasks would be conducted in the world outside the school, and make sense to students.

Formative evaluation is evaluation based on data collected before the instructional unit is completed. When you gather assessment data during a lesson, chapter, or curriculum unit, that data can be used to help develop the remainder of the instructional cycle.

Informal assessment is also used to refer to nontraditional assessment practices. This term emphasizes the informal and ongoing nature of the ways in which data may be collected in contrast to the formality of a written exam. This informality makes it easier for assessment strategies to be incorporated into the instructional process.

Outcomes, such as "organizing and interpreting data," are broad abilities around which curriculum and lessons are developed. These "big ideas" define what is important to be learned and, therefore, assessed.

Performance assessment is yet another term used to refer to alternative assessment practices. This terms emphasizes the active nature of assessment tasks. For example, we can find out what students know about measuring by observing them perform measurement tasks.

Summative evaluation is evaluation that is conducted immediately after the instructional unit is completed. A unit test, a chapter test, and completed projects are examples of this type of evaluation. Summative evaluation is used to measure student learning and, at times, the appropriateness of the instructional techniques and materials.

Why do we need new assessment strategies?

Think about one child in your classroom. Write down the child's name. Think about the child in relationship to mathematics. Try to visualize that child learning and using mathematics in your classroom. Now imagine that the child's family is moving out-of-state. What could you tell the new teacher about the child's learning of mathematics? What new mathematical ideas is the child developing? What mathematical ideas has the child mastered? What are the child's strengths in mathematics? weaknesses? How does the child best learn mathematics? Does the child like mathematics? Does the child like exploring mathematical ideas with others? Make a list of any thoughts that come to mind. Once your brainstorming has been completed, read the items on your list. As you read each item ask yourself, How do I know this?

Chances are that your sources of knowledge were varied. You probably didn't rely solely on the child's performance on tests. Perhaps you remembered the child working with others, saying something in the school yard, solving a problem, or asking a question. You had multiple sources of information, which when taken together, helped you form a picture of the child as a learner and user of mathematics. For years, many elementary school teachers have used such sources of information to understand their students more fully, but educators have not always considered such sources to be legitimate assessment strategies. This is changing.

Nationally, increased attention is being given to ways that mathematical learning is assessed. This interest is being fueled by many factors, including:

- New standards for the teaching of mathematics.
- A strengthened belief that instruction and assessment should be more closely linked.
- A new understanding of the way in which students learn.
- An increased concern for equity.
- Continued pressure for accountability.

Perhaps most important, teachers and school systems have expressed an interest in learning more about assessment strategies.

Standards

This is an exciting time to be involved in teaching mathematics. *Curriculum and Evaluation Standards for the Teaching of School Mathematics* (NCTM 1989) and its companion document, *Professional Standards for the Teaching of Mathematics* (NCTM 1991), provide a new vision for the learning and teaching of mathematics. These volumes emphasize mathematics instruction that focuses on meaningful mathematical inquiry. The goals of such inquiry are to help students:

- Learn to solve problems.
- Communicate with and about mathematics.
- Reason mathematically.
- Make connections within mathematics and between mathematics and other subject areas.
- Value mathematics.

These goals represent big ideas, ones that will continue to develop throughout a student's education. Since they are different from specific skill-based outcomes, evaluation of these outcomes differs as well.

Traditionally, teachers have relied heavily on paper-and-pencil tests to assess their students' knowledge of mathematics. These tests generally contain questions, often written in a multiple-choice format, that have one numerical answer. Such a format involves recognizing or responding to answers rather than constructing them. Teachers often give these tests at the end of a week, chapter, or curriculum unit. Used in this way, they are forms of summative evaluation. While these tests may be used less frequently in the early elementary grades, workbooks and blackline masters contain similar types of questions.

Although questions like these may be appropriate for assessing the learning of isolated skills, they are not appropriate for assessing the more process-centered goals of the new standards. These goals are broad-based and need to be assessed through more open-ended tasks. Multiple perspectives, not multiple choices, are required. Further, since these goal-related abilities develop over long periods of time, they also require ongoing assessment.

Linking instruction and assessment

Assessment tasks must be aligned with the goals and pedagogical styles of the curriculum. It is not appropriate to teach according to one set of goals, strategies, and beliefs and evaluate according to another set. We do not teach people to drive on a country lane and then assess their learning by asking them to drive on city streets. Rather, we observe them driving on similar country lanes.

However, if passing a driving test on city streets is the goal, that is where some of the learning and practice must occur. We need to link our classroom assessment practices and our instructional practices in the same manner. In this way, we can get a fairer indication of what our students have learned and can make better instructional decisions based on results of the assessment tasks we use.

For example, in *Curriculum and Evaluation Standards for School Mathematics*, the development of mathematical power is identified as a goal of mathematics instruction. The document links this notion to assessment by stating:

> The assessment of students' mathematical knowledge should yield information about their—
> * Ability to apply their knowledge to solve problems within mathematics and other disciplines;
> * Ability to use mathematical language to communicate ideas;
> * Ability to reason and analyze;
> * Knowledge and understanding of concepts and procedures;
> * Disposition toward mathematics;
> * Understanding of the nature of mathematics;
> * Integration of these aspects of mathematics knowledge. (NTCM 1989, p. 205)

As we focus on new aspects of mathematics, our assessment strategies will need to change. For example, if we want to assess our students' abilities to communicate mathematically, then we must use assessment strategies that provide opportunities for students to write and talk about mathematics.

NCTM recognizes the importance of further linking instruction to assessment and is in the process of developing a third volume, *Assessment Standards for School Mathematics*, to complement its existing two volumes. Its working draft (NCTM 1993) identifies six assessment standards:

* Important mathematics.
* Enhanced learning.
* Equity.
* Openness.
* Valid inferences.
* Consistency.

These standards provide criteria against which an assessment task can be judged. The first two speak directly to the relationship between instruction and assessment. The first, important mathematics, states that assessment tasks must represent the big ideas of mathematics, those considered important for students to learn. The second, enhanced learning, states that assessment tasks must also be thought of as learning and teaching tools. Such tasks should engage students in meaningful tasks and be part of normal daily classroom practice.

Consider the work of first grader Todd shown in Figure 1–1. He was asked to write about the heights of the people in his family. Todd's teacher was surprised that he knew such specific data and asked him about it. Todd explained that his family had recently been to an amusement park that required children to be a minimum height of four feet in order to go on certain rides. There was

FIGURE 1–1.　*Todd's Observations About Height*

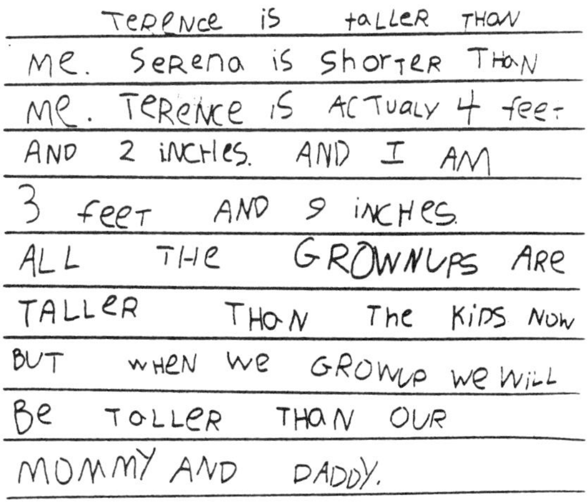

> TeReNce is taLLeR THaN
> me. SeReNa is ShorTeR THaN
> me. TeReNce is ACTualy 4 feet
> AND 2 iNcHes. AND I AM
> 3 feeT AND 9 iNcHes.
> ALL THe GR∅WNUPs ARe
> TALLeR THa N The KiDS Now
> BUT wHeN we GROWUp we Will
> Be TOLLeR THaN OUR
> MOMMY AND DADDY.

a vertical measuring stick at the entrance to these rides. All of the children in Todd's family had been measured. Only Todd's older brother met the minimum standard.

Todd's work shows that he is able to communicate quite fluently. His ability to form sentences and spell correctly is quite remarkable for a child of his age. He correctly uses the terms *shorter* and *taller* and the units *feet* and *inches*. His assumption that eventually all of the children will be taller than their parents may be naive, but may also indicate a delightful hopefulness in light of the fact that Todd did not yet meet the minimum standard. Most important, Todd's work shows the level of detail that children can remember when the mathematics involved is relevant to their real-world experiences.

How students learn

Not only has there been a rethinking about the mathematical concepts students should learn, but there is also a new understanding of how students learn. Cognitive psychologists continue to help all of us understand more about the learning process. Recently, there has been new interest in the idea that children construct their own meanings. Students do not passively absorb information; they approach a new situation with prior knowledge. As they assimilate new information, they form their own meanings. Since students are involved in the process of constructing and connecting ideas, it is important that we provide learning activities that have meaningful and interesting contexts and that place students in active roles. Consider the following example.

Asham, a second-grade teacher, helped his students make a graph of the number of students who were present and absent each day of school. Each month the students reviewed and interpreted the data. They discussed patterns as well as possible reasons for the patterns. During the winter months two important events affected the rate of attendance. There was an unexpected and serious snowstorm that started around 5:00 a. m. one day in March. Although school was not canceled, many parents decided to keep their children home. In fact, more than half of the children were not in class. That day had the highest absence rate of the year. In January, there was a serious outbreak of the flu, which passed through the classroom from one child to another. For two weeks in a row, there were five or six children absent every day. The data for both of these events looked very different from the other data.

One day when the children were discussing a graph they had made showing the weight of their dogs, one child said, "This dog is much heavier than the others. It is like our snowstorm day." Asham then pointed to the bars representing two dogs that were heavier than all the other dogs but not as heavy as the dog that the child had identified and asked, "Are these dogs heavy too?" The child responded, "Yes, but like when everyone had the flu, not the snowstorm day." From that day on, the class referred to outliers as "like the snowstorm day" and data that were different but not extreme as "like when everyone had the flu." The children had found a meaningful context in which to develop these ideas and had constructed their own language for discussing them. It is within this meaningful context that information is stored and remembered. Over time, the ideas will be revisited and become more sophisticated.

This view of learning changes the role of the teacher from one of provider of all knowledge to facilitator of all activities. Students have a corresponding change in role; they must be actively involved in investigations in order to gain a meaningful understanding of mathematical ideas. To understand what our students are thinking, we must have access to their expression of ideas. Consider this example.

John has a dog who lost a leg to cancer. John says it is incredibly interesting to take a walk with a three-legged dog—you learn a lot about people. Young children are particularly interested in what happened to the dog and are quite open about asking questions. Older children are impressed with how fast she can still run and wonder about how the way she moves now compares with the way she moved when she had four legs. Almost everyone is surprised to hear that it took her so little time to learn how to walk with three legs. In fact, she walked out of the operating room.

One of John's favorite stories involves two four-year-old boys. One petted the dog while the other walked around her, looking inquisitively at her body. He bent his head down more and circled her a second time. Finally he looked up and asked, "Where does she keep her fourth leg?" "She doesn't have one," John replied. "She lost it." The boy thought for a moment, scratched his head, and said, "Do you think she'll ever find it?"

The first question is not, what happened to the fourth leg? but, where is it kept? The child's previous knowledge tells him that all dogs have four legs. Therefore, this dog must have four legs . . . so where is it? Also, the euphemistic use of the term lost is not familiar to the child. As he understands the term, it is possible to find things that are lost. Given his experience, his thinking is perfectly reasonable. Yet few of us would have predicted this response. Only through conversation was it possible to gain these important insights into the child's thinking.

As teachers, you probably have many similar stories about students who said things that you did not expect. Often it is the most surprising and humorous remarks that you remember. But you gain insights into your students' thinking every day—though all those insights may not be equally memorable—by actively listening to your students. In fact, one of the most important aspects of your role as a teacher is to orchestrate the discourse in your classroom. You need to pose interesting questions, ask students to clarify their ideas, monitor student participation, and decide when your input is needed. By providing your students with tasks that give them opportunities to clarify their thinking about mathematics, you are also providing yourself with ongoing assessment data.

Equity

When one assessment strategy is used almost exclusively, the information learned is severely limited. Further, the strategy may have a built-in bias toward a particular style of learning. For example, a student may have a better understanding of geometric terms when she encounters them in context than she demonstrates when asked to match terms with their definitions out of context. If assessment strategies employed in this student's classroom involve the matching technique only, the student's understanding will be assessed as low. However, if multiple assessment strategies are used, the student will have the opportunity to demonstrate her strengths.

In order to ensure that assessment strategies are equitable, each student should be held to high expectations and helped to meet those expectations. Assessments should be designed to allow the students to demonstrate what they know, not to determine what they don't know. Take a minute to reflect on equity issues related to your classroom by considering these questions:

- Do I use several assessments as evidence of learning?
- Do my assessment tasks involve a variety of contexts, cultural references, and response modes?
- How could my school help me modify assessments to meet the different learning needs of the students in my classroom?
- Is assessment viewed as part of the multicultural agenda of my school?

Since your students have many different previous experiences, cultures, and learning styles, you may find it helpful to involve other professionals in the assessment process—a committee or study group from your school, town, professional group, or local college or another teacher in your school. Whatever the format, working with others will expose you to different perspectives and help you better meet the diverse needs of your students.

NCTM identifies equity as its third assessment standard. In its working draft it states:

> Every assessment activity must be measured against the equity standard. All of those involved in mathematics assessments must consciously attend to equity. Even as professionals disagree on descriptions and means of achieving equity, its place as a standard is not in doubt and must not be compromised or devalued. (NCTM 1993, 39)

Accountability

A climate of accountability is also bringing increased attention to assessment. Given the economic reality of our times, demands for accountability will continue. The public has a right to be assured that their tax dollars are yielding results, and parents have the right to know that their children are learning. As teachers, we are under pressure to produce results.

Standardized tests are often norm-referenced—that is, they are designed to rank students with respect to a particular trait or ability. Such a test assumes a normal population and is used to identify where within the population a particular student falls. It generally uses a format that focuses on the ability of the student to recognize the correct answer within a list of choices. This type of test suggests several attitudes toward mathematics and the learning of mathematics that are no longer held. For example:

- Reporting one score for mathematics suggests that mathematics is a single domain.
- Basing a score on one or two hours of student work suggests that students' work is consistent at all times.
- Using a multiple-choice format suggests that recognition of the correct answer is all that is important.

Standardized testing, however, is not going to go away. In fact, 77 percent of the public is in favor of standardized testing in our schools (Finn 1991). At the same time, the focus on accountability has brought the composition of current standardized tests into question. The College Board has made several changes recently. The Scholastic Achievement Tests (SATs) are now known as the Scholastic Assessment Tests, the use of calculators is allowed, and sections with student-generated answers are included.

Many states are beginning to develop different kinds of test questions and different types of testing situations. Maine and New York, for instance, provide certain manipulative materials, such as counters and rulers, to be used while taking the tests. Exams in states such as California, Kentucky, Massachusetts, and Maine include open-ended questions that can be solved in different ways and that require students to explain their mathematical thinking.

For years many teachers complained that they wanted to give more time to the teaching of problem solving but felt they had to continue to emphasize basic skills, because basic skills were emphasized on standardized tests. Ironically, the new state standardized tests are now becoming the impetus for a greater focus on problem solving in classroom instruction and assessment practices. If "the test" focuses on the development of problem solving, reasoning, communicating, connecting, and valuing mathematics, is teaching to the test such a bad thing?

What is alternative assessment and what does it involve?

Having explored the need for new assessment strategies, we want to focus on these strategies. Many terms are used to refer to new assessment practices: *alternative assessment, authentic assessment, informal assessment* and *performance assessment* are often used interchangeably. In general, they are used in contrast to the traditional testing practices that emphasize paper-and-pencil formats and that are often standardized and written in a multiple-choice format. Because the tests are standardized or normed, they are usually used to compare students, towns, or states with one another. They provide a rank order. Many teachers dread the week of standardized testing. They know that many of their students will become tired and irritable. The "Do Not Disturb" sign posted on the classroom door during such times illustrates how different the testing period behavior is from normal classroom behavior. Although some school systems may use data from standardized tests to group children, teachers rarely use such test scores to plan their lessons.

Alternative assessment practices do not take place during a specifically designated class period or week, but are integrated into the instructional practices of the classroom. The term *informal assessment* emphasizes this characteristic. Since the assessments can be conducted informally, they can be fully integrated into the curriculum and provide ongoing information about what students are learning. Since these assessments are integrated into the curriculum, they must be aligned with the content and assessment goals of the curriculum and the way in which the curriculum is delivered. If students learn by working in cooperative groups, using manipulatives, and having calculators and computers available to them, then this instructional environment should also be available during assessments. The term *authentic assessment* emphasizes that assessment tasks must authentically represent the way in which the learning has been conducted, be worthwhile, and represent the way in which the tasks would be conducted in the world outside school. The real world is also emphasized in the term *performance evaluation*. To know mathematics is to do mathematics, to perform it in a real-word situation.

Consider a couple of classroom snapshots.

Martin teaches kindergarten. He is interacting with one of his students, Sarita, at the sand table. He shows Sarita two containers and asks which one will hold more sand. Here's part of their conversation:

MARTIN: Which will hold more sand, this blue can or this red can?
SARITA: The red one.
MARTIN: How do you know?
SARITA: Because it is taller.
MARTIN: Will taller containers always hold more sand?
SARITA: Yup. Taller means bigger.
MARTIN: Is there a way that you can show me that the red one holds more sand than the blue one?
SARITA: Sure. Look. [*Sarita places the red and blue containers side by side. She points to the top of the blue container showing that it is shorter than the red one.*] This one is bigger.

Martin notes that Sarita does not recognize the three dimensions of volume, but rather focuses on height. He decides he will organize some activities for her that require her to fill tall and thin containers with sand and then pour that sand into containers that are shorter but hold more sand. Martin will then talk with Sarita again to see if these experiences change her thinking.

Kathy teaches the fourth grade. She asks her students how they know that $4 \times 9 = 36$:

STACEY: Because nine and nine and nine and nine are thirty-six.
LOUIE: Well, four times ten is forty and four less is thirty-six.

Josh: I know that two times nine is eighteen and if I add nine, then it's twenty-seven and then another nine is thirty-six.
Kathy: Does anyone have any other ideas?
Katrina: I could add four together nine times, but that would take a long time.
Marisa: I know that nine and nine is eighteen. Then I can double that to get thirty-six.

Kathy then asks her students to work in pairs to record the different ways they know that $5 \times 6 = 30$. She is pleased that her students understand the meaning of multiplication as repeated addition and generally have good thinking strategies for multiplication facts. Kathy reads the students' recordings to note the accuracy of their techniques, their ability to communicate the techniques, and the number and variety of techniques they generate. She decides that most of her students are ready to explore the use of mathematical symbols to communicate these techniques. She has identified a small group of students, however, that need to do some activity cards highlighting thinking strategies.

How will alternative assessment strategies change my mathematics teaching?

Alternative assessment techniques make use of things you are already doing: the notes you record about your students, the observations of your students you make every day. They also give you the opportunity to plan your teaching differently, to identify broad learning outcomes rather than a list of specific behavioral objectives as curricular goals. Using alternative assessments prompts you to think more explicitly about how you will recognize when students have met those outcomes. For instance, how do students demonstrate that they understand graphs? What do students do when they are just beginning to develop this concept? are working on this concept? have mastered it? These "performance indicators" are explained more fully in Chapter 2.

Many of the ways you find evidence of student learning are validated within this model of assessment. You are not limited to student tests, but can include student portfolios, journals, projects, responses to open-ended questions, interviews, self- and peer assessments, and your observations of students as sources of evidence. Most likely, you will need to reflect on how to interpret that evidence and find ways to record it that are meaningful and manageable.

Most important, this new view of assessment makes formative evaluation integral to the instructional process. You use the assessment data to direct or modify your lesson planning. This is sometimes referred to as *informing* instruction. Again, this is a process that you are already practicing daily. Think of how often you extend your lesson plans because of student interest. You often redirect a student with your questions or decide to use a different approach to teach a new idea. You make these decisions "on your feet" because of good teacher instincts. By using alternative assessment techniques you will more clearly understand why you are making these decisions and be better able to articulate them. Since you will have more meaningful assessment data available to you, you will be better able to communicate to your students, their parents, your principal, and the community at large about learning goals and progress in your classroom.

This clear articulation allows students to understand your expectations better and helps involve them in their own learning. It helps your colleagues gain a better understanding of your educational goals and thus be more able to support them. This model of the assessment cycle is summarized in Figure 1–2.

You may be wondering if you must always use alternative assessment strategies. Traditional tests and performance-based assessments are different ways of acquiring information about how children think and what they have learned. There are times when multiple-choice tests are quite appropriate. When you are assessing a child's knowledge of multiplication facts or vocabulary, a multiple-choice format may be the most beneficial because it efficiently measures learning of relatively uncomplicated information. However, when you want to gather information on how students understand more complex concepts, such as place value, forms of alternative assessment are the better choice. They provide a deeper, richer look at students' thinking.

Finally, assessment is not an end goal, but a means to achieving instructional outcomes. By incorporating new assessment strategies into your teaching, you may find that it will:

- Become more focused on broad outcomes like the NCTM standards.
- Use performance indicators as benchmarks for student learning.
- Include assessment strategies that provide new sources of evidence of student learning and that allow all students to demonstrate what they know.
- Help your students gain more control of their learning.
- Be informed in an ongoing manner through your assessment data.
- Provide information on student learning to students, parents, and administrators that is rich in description about the developing abilities of your students.

FIGURE 1–2. *Model of the Assessment Cycle*

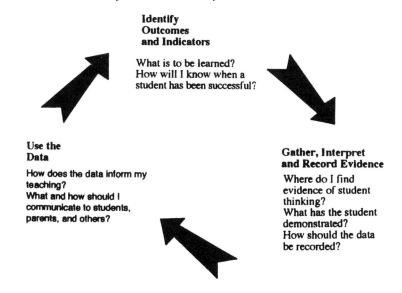

How can this book help me use new assessment strategies in my classroom?

First of all, we want to help you see the relationship between theory and practice. A theoretical framework for assessment is provided in connection with specific examples—classroom vignettes and samples of children's work. We hope these examples give you a picture of what alternative assessment practices look like and how they might look in your classroom.

Second, we believe that learning is an active process. Thus, there are times when we ask you to record your thoughts, brainstorm ideas, or react to student work. Ideally, you will read this book along with a colleague. The opportunity to talk with a peer about issues related to assessment is very helpful.

Third, we want you to have access to other information about assessment. As with most theoretical topics, there are many terms associated with it. Each chapter includes a list of key terms, and these lists are combined into a single glossary in the appendix.

Finally, as a preview to help you focus your reading, each chapter begins by listing the key questions that will be addressed.

· 2 ·

Identifying Abilities We Value

For so long I have depended on the textbook to give me a sense of what I should be teaching. Now the NCTM standards *are suggesting another way to think about what I need to emphasize in my mathematics lessons. I'm not quite sure what the important ideas are that my students need to be learning and how I know when they have really learned those ideas.*

In This Chapter

♦ What are the NCTM standards?
♦ How do the curriculum and evaluation standards help us translate what is valued in mathematics to instruction?
♦ How do the NCTM standards build on what we know about how children learn?
♦ In what mathematical abilities do we want elementary students to experience success?
♦ What is the role of performance indicators in bringing together instruction and assessment?
♦ How do I determine performance indicators?
♦ How will identifying performance indicators affect my teaching?

Key Terms

A conceptual map is a graphic representation of the interrelationship of skills and abilities a particular standard of content may comprise. It depicts this interrelationship as a network of related abilities or concepts.

Standards are public statements about what is valued in a curriculum. Standards define locally, statewide, or nationally what will be emphasized in a particular subject without specifying exactly how it will be taught.

Content standards are specific curricular outcomes that have been identified as essential to mathematical literacy. Each of the thirteen NCTM curriculum and evaluation standards is a content standard.

Performance standards are descriptive statements that make clear what a student needs to do in order to provide evidence of having learned a specific content standard. Performance standards help answer a question such as, How do we know a student is a successful problem solver in mathematics?

Performance indicators give an idea of what student success looks like in terms of content and performance standards. The descriptions often reflect a continuum of development.

Behavioral objectives provide a detailed set of benchmarks, based on grade level, indicating students' mastery of specified procedural skills (addition facts, for example). Traditionally, curriculums were written based on the assumption that a child with average abilities might achieve stated objectives at certain grade levels and periods of time within a grade level.

What are the NCTM standards?

The National Council of Teachers of Mathematics' *Curriculum and Evaluation and Professional Teaching Standards* suggest that school mathematics should emphasize certain standards in content and performance in kindergarten through high school. In this instance, the meaning of the term *standard* is quite different from that implied in the concept of standardized testing. Whereas standardized tests involve a uniform testing situation, standards are statements that describe what should be valued in mathematics education. The NCTM standards have been agreed to by teachers of mathematics, curriculum developers, specialists in learning and development, and mathematicians. Consensus among this diverse group of professionals about what should be valued in school mathematics makes the *Curriculum and Evaluation Standards and Professional Teaching Standards* unique documents, bringing together what we know about mathematics, how teaching can support these standards, how children learn, and what abilities children will need across their life spans and using this knowledge to guide all educators in the direction of common instructional goals.

On a very general level the NCTM's *Curriculum and Evaluation Standards* provides a framework of concepts, or "big ideas," that identifies elements in mathematics believed to be key to understanding and applying mathematics in everyday life. The standards emphasize the importance of having students build an understanding of concepts like measurement, number sense, probability, and spatial visualization. At the same time the standards acknowledge that this understanding takes time and developmental maturity to achieve and that cognitive understanding may develop at different rates among children.

For this reason, the standards do not look the same at each grade level. They are organized across three grade clusters, K–4, 5–8, and 9–12. In this way, each teacher at each grade level contributes to a child's mathematical development. (The curriculum standards for grades K–8 are shown in Figure 2–1.)

How do the NCTM curriculum and evaluation standards help us translate what is valued in mathematics to instruction?

The oft-encountered phrase urging teachers to "link assessment to instruction" means that instruction and assessment should be closely aligned and that good instructional tasks can also be good assessment tasks. The verb *to link* gives us permission to recognize student evaluation as integral in helping to achieve instructional goals, rather than as separate from instruction. The standards have succeeded in shaping two closely related themes that make a critical contribution to our ability to link instruction with assessment. First, they have replaced behavioral objectives as the primary tool in curriculum planning. Further, the standards suggest that a mathematics curriculum should be organized around concepts or big ideas, not only the acquisition of vocabulary, procedural skills, or algorithms.

The NCTM standards are quite different from the behavioral objectives taught in traditional education methods courses. Behavioral objectives are statements about the discrete skills a child is expected to learn within a specified span of time, at a particular grade level. For example, a behavioral objective might state that a child should be able to count forward and backward between one and one hundred by the end of first grade or know the multiplication tables through the nines by the middle of the fourth grade. Behavioral objectives provide teachers with a detailed set of benchmarks, based on grade-level, indicating students' mastery of specified procedural skills. For years, it has been assumed

FIGURE 2–1. *NCTM Curriculum Standards for School Mathematics for Grades K–Eight*

Grades K–Four	Grades 5–8
1. Mathematics as Problem Solving	1. Mathematics as Problem Solving
2. Mathematics as Communications	2. Mathematics as Communications
3. Mathematics as Reasoning	3. Mathematics as Reasoning
4. Mathematical Connections	4. Mathematical Connections
5. Estimation	5. Number and Number Relationships
6. Number Sense and Numeration	6. Number Systems and Number Theory
7. Concepts of Whole Number Operations	7. Computation and Estimation
8. Whole Number Computation	8. Patterns and Functions
9. Geometry and Spatial Sense	9. Algebra
10. Measurement	10. Statistics
11. Statistics and Probability	11. Probability
12. Fractions and Decimals	12. Geometry
13. Patterns and Relationships	13. Measurement

that these benchmarks represented skills that a child with average abilities might achieve, and that on average, most children would conform to the suggested timetable and grade level for attainment of these skills.

The NCTM curriculum and evaluation standards suggest a different picture. Whereas behavioral objectives focus on the acquisition of basic skills as the primary goal for mathematics, the standards identify certain conceptual and content knowledge as key to students' understanding and using mathematics in everyday life. For example, the standard for number sense states that across the kindergarten-through-fourth-grade time span the mathematics curriculum should include consistent learning experiences that help a student understand our numeration system by relating counting, grouping, and place value concepts.

Think about the significant differences between behavioral objectives and curriculum standards. First, these differences clearly reveal a significant shift in the organization of a mathematics curriculum. Where traditional elementary mathematics was organized around the manner in which textbooks presented topics like addition and subtraction, emerging curriculum frameworks are organized around much broader concepts like problem solving and number sense. Second, these differences allow us to rethink the role of time in the instructional process. A behavioral-objective approach dictates a procedural skill to be acquired by a student by a particular point in time; a standard describes the acquisition of broader, conceptual outcomes based on a number of abilities that a child can develop with increasing complexity across grade levels.

Acknowledging that children need time to grasp central mathematical ideas gives us permission to develop lessons other than those focusing solely on the acquisition of mathematics algorithms or facts or the computation of numbers. Instead, we can develop lessons that incorporate discovery of algorithms in the context of learning about larger mathematical ideas in projects or investigations developed over a span of two or three days or extending over a number of weeks or possibly months.

How do the NCTM standards build on what we know about how children learn?

Organizing school mathematics around concepts supports what is known in cognitive psychology about children's need to be active participants in their learning. Children store information and understanding in large cognitive networks. This network is naturally organized around big ideas, which for mathematics includes categories such as problem solving, patterns and functions of numbers, spatial visualization, and whole number operations. As you visualize this network, think about the pattern in a spiderweb or in a volleyball net and how that pattern might apply to a conceptual map your students construct in class. The conceptual map in Figure 2–2 was constructed by sixth grader Douglas to represent his current understanding of measurement.

At any given time we have within our mental structures a weblike pattern formed from in-school and out-of-school experiences. Each central point in this network of mental activity represents our conceptual understanding of ideas like measurement, which grows more abstract and complex with maturity and cumulative learning experiences. Take a few moments and represent your under-

FIGURE 2–2.   *Student Representation of Measurement*

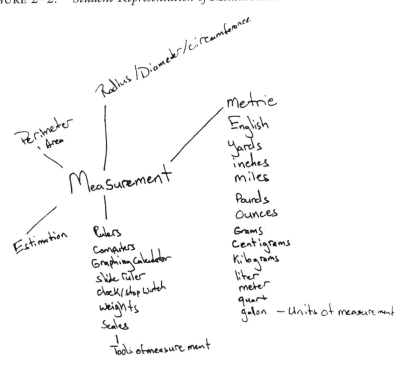

standing of measurement. Ask yourself, When I think of measurement, what do I think of?

Everyone organizes information and experiences around these concepts in a way that has meaning even if it contains misconceptions. Cognitive networks are built over time, from experiences and information that "make sense" to us, even if that sense making is not 100 percent accurate. In fact, because it *is not* always 100 percent accurate we need to build in instructional opportunities that will inform us of student misconceptions and that will allow our students to communicate their understanding to one another. It is in this process of sharing that differences in understanding are discovered. These differences can be critical, because what may initially appear to be a misunderstanding is not necessarily a misunderstanding. A child may simply be using different words to describe an understanding that is quite sound, but that we hear as incorrect because of the vocabulary.

A teacher's role, then, is not to give the correct answers but to allow children the time and opportunity to build up their understanding of mathematics through contextualized problems that make sense to them and that provide opportunities for the teacher to gather information on student progress toward assimilating key mathematical ideas. The cognitive work of children actively engaged in understanding new ideas or fitting new information into previous ideas is made easier when they can recognize where in the web or map this new information belongs. It is also much more helpful for a student to learn new concepts when the related examples or tasks involve everyday situations that mean something to the student. Situations in which children have an opportunity to work with and practice mathematics in ways that make sense to them play an important role in properly channeling new information within their cognitive networks.

The conceptual-network model is very different from how we used to think information was stored and retrieved. Previously it was assumed that information was stored in a much more linear pattern, as if in a file cabinet, and that understanding came from the accumulation in a single "file" of discrete pieces of information about a larger topic. The goal was to provide students with as many "pieces" as possible—dates, names, vocabulary, and procedural skills—so that these could be "called up" or "pulled out" of the file when necessary. Many of our traditional testing practices reflect this idea of calling up the right answer from such a file as evidence of understanding.

Two ways to learn to find the area of a rectangle

Think for a moment about the way in which you learned to find the area of a rectangle. You probably first memorized the algorithm of base times height as the right way to find the solution. In order to practice this formula, you applied it to a series of rectangles of varying size. The application of the formula to many rectangles was a way to assure teachers and parents that you had "learned the formula," that it had been filed away in the appropriate folder and could be called up on demand.

Another approach to learning how to find the area of a rectangle is to let students discover the formula themselves. First, the students use geoboards and geobands to create a series of rectangles. After a period of exploration, they transfer their figures from the geoboards to graph or grid paper. They then have an array of data available about the length, width, and number of spaces contained in specific rectangles, which can be displayed on an overhead or a chalkboard. Through class discussion, the students look for patterns that might lead to a formula for finding the area of a rectangle, testing their conjectures as a class. Individual students will probably express this formula in different ways, using different words, but it is in essence the same formula.

One fourth-grade student whose teacher had just gone through this process explained the day's lesson this way:

> We made some rectangles today. The teacher said to count the spaces in between. Like the length is 4 and the width is 3, then the area is 12. Then we did a paper to do different rectangles that we did before. Then after that the teacher asked for a formula or a pattern. Mike, Anna, and Gillian found a formula. Mike's formula was length × width = area. Anna's formula was columns × rows = area. Gillian's formula was L × W = A. L is length. Width is W and A is area. This can help you with multiplication.

The accumulative model of learning—a file cabinet in which algorithms are stored away after practicing the procedures repeatedly—may be effective for the short term, but it is not compatible with long-term memory. When information is learned out of context, it is not remembered over time. Concepts need to be learned gradually, shaped and constructed through many learning experiences that involve guided exploration. Also, it is becoming increasingly clear that with so many "bits" of information in the world about various subjects, teaching all such "bits" to students is an impossible goal.

Our current understanding of how learning occurs supports students' developing larger conceptualizations (like the search for patterns described in the lesson on rectangles) rather than memorizing discrete pieces of information. However, remember that a conceptual understanding of mathematics, built up over time, does *not* mean that students will not need to know algorithms or basic mathematical skills like multiplication tables. These kinds of mathematics skills will remain necessary to some degree, but other instruction focused on discovery, conceptual understanding, and application will provide a cognitive anchor for these skills.

In which mathematical abilities do we want elementary students to experience success?

NCTM has developed thirteen curriculum standards or outcomes for kindergarten through fourth grade and for grades five through eight (they are listed in Figure 2–1). If you review these standards, you will find that some of the outcomes for these two grade clusters are the same and some are different. Problem solving and mathematical connections are examples of process-like outcomes that are shared across the grades. Algebra is not introduced until grades five through eight, but outcomes for kindergarten through four, like patterns and relationships, prepare students for ideas central to algebra.

For teachers to integrate these standards into their mathematics classes, they must identify the skills and abilities their students need to practice in order to achieve the standards. Defining such skills and abilities in conjunction with colleagues is an important first step in creating an instructional bridge between the larger, conceptual outcomes identified in the standards and the kinds of instruction and assessment necessary to support student acquisition of those outcomes. How likely are you to find time to have these kinds of critical discussions? At the very least it may be possible to have informal conversations with at least one other colleague in your building. At most, you may be able to develop a formal strategy for these discussions, perhaps a series of ongoing inservice days or a designated segment of grade-level meetings.

By yourself or with a colleague, try the following brainstorming exercise. Can you visualize students who have been successful problem solvers? As you get a mental image of these students, place them in a problem-solving situation. Can you jot down the learner behaviors you associate with being a successful problem solver? After you have written those behaviors down, study them. Ask yourself whether there are any connections among these learner behaviors. For example, can you build a conceptual map from these behaviors with problem solving at the center? Some of the behaviors that might come to mind are devising a problem-solving strategy, revising an initial strategy based on information discovered during the problem-solving process, or explaining why a problem-solving strategy is effective.

The list in Figure 2–3 was produced during a brainstorming session about good problem-solving abilities relative to a particular fourth-grade class. Figure

FIGURE 2–3. *"What does a successful problem solver do?"*

Brainstorms well

Sees patterns in problem types

Tries out a strategy both as an individual and as a member of a group

Puts together questions about the problem

Uses a variety of strategies

Can explain a problem solving strategy orally and in writing

Understands an unreasonable solution

Demonstrates self-confidence in the problem solving process

Gathers a lot of information or data

2–4 expands on this list and configures it as a conceptual map. Depending on the grade level or age of the child you are envisioning, your list of learner abilities may differ both in the language used to describe them and in their degree of sophistication. Overall, though, there will be some overlap. In fact, we recommend trying this exercise with a teacher who is at a different grade level. First, jot down behaviors separately and then discuss each of your lists, noting similarities and differences as well as the language you used to describe learner behaviors.

FIGURE 2–4. *Conceptual Map of Problem Solving*

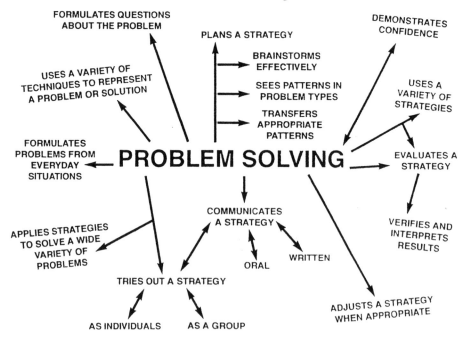

Identifying abilities that suggest students have a good sense of numbers is particularly challenging, so let's look at an example of that as well. Suppose one of your students has created and completed the following addition problem:

$$
\begin{array}{r}
10 \\
+\ 632 \\
+\ \ \ 8 \\
\hline
1532
\end{array}
$$

Does this student have good number sense? Why? Why not? Does this example give you ideas for talking to your students about number sense? Take time to write down your thoughts. Examples similar to this one taken from your own classroom experiences are a very helpful basis for setting instructional goals and developing assessment criteria. They are concrete examples of what the larger conceptual ideas in the NCTM's standards documents mean in your own classroom. Using student products provides you with very clear examples of student thinking and is thus a way to verify that your students are in fact developing the kinds of skills you would like them to be developing, ones you feel are important. Figure 2–5 lists abilities a group of teachers brainstormed relative to number sense.

What is the role of performance indicators in bringing together instruction and assessment?

When you broke down problem-solving behaviors by brainstorming what good problem solving looks like or thought about what constitutes good number sense, you took an initial step in identifying and working on performance standards. Performance standards provide an overview of what a student needs to do in order to achieve success in an identified content standard.

Content standards refer to outcomes believed to be essential to mathematical literacy. Each of the thirteen NCTM curriculum and evaluation standards is a content standard; taken as a whole they reflect what is now believed to be the essential "content" of school mathematics. Performance standards, by contrast,

FIGURE 2–5. *Student Abilities Relative to Number Sense*

Understands numbers are symbols
Uses numbers to quantify
Devlops an intuition about numbers
Understands number meanings and patterns
Knows when a number is an estimate
Uses numbers to identify a specific object in a collection
Uses thinking strategies in computation
Understands the magnitude of numbers
Uses numbers to measure
Understands the relationships among numbers

are descriptive statements that make clear what a student needs to do as evidence that she has learned a specific content standard. For example, for the problem-solving content standard, using a problem-solving strategy in a variety of mathematical contexts may be one of the standards of performance you build into your mathematics lessons and, consequently, use to assess your students' ability to be good problem solvers in mathematics. Many states are now developing statewide curriculum frameworks that identify both content and performance standards.

How do I determine performance indicators?

Having selected the content standards that will be your instructional focus in mathematics and developed the performance standards that specify the broad abilities that make up those content standards, the next step is to develop specific performance indicators—criteria that describe a continuum of learner development in a specified ability.

Again, try to visualize your responses to these questions:

- If a student was just learning how to communicate a problem-solving strategy in writing, what would he say?
- If a student was accomplished at writing about a problem-solving strategy, what would she say?
- If a student was somewhere between these two extremes, what might he say? (For example, a student may be able to describe what strategy was chosen, but may not be able to enumerate all the steps involved.)

Benchmarks at these three levels are *indicators* of your students' *performance* with regard to communicating in writing about problem solving; hence, the term *performance indicators*. These indicators provide criteria against which to assess your students both in their everyday lessons and in more formal situations.

Now take another performance standard for problem solving, like identifying problem types, and think about what performance indicators might look like at your grade level. Your continuum might look something like the one in Figure 2–6.

Performance standards and indicators are as important for assessment as they are for instruction. They target for teachers, students, parents, and administrators, in very concrete ways, what is valued in mathematics. The lessons you develop as a teacher should allow students to practice identified performance standards. You can then observe that practice through informal assessment, provide feedback to your students, and use this information to adjust future instruction and create more formal assessment situations.

One note of caution. Determining performance indicators and criteria may be the most difficult aspect of the process of assessment. It certainly has been for us in working with groups of teachers across the country. You will be tempted to stop too soon, before you have clearly articulated the criteria or performance indicators you believe are most appropriate for your students. A standard as broad as problem solving may require a number of descriptive statements (criteria) to capture what you believe to be the essential performance standards and an appropriate range of performance indicators for those standards. Also, your descriptive statements must capture the essence of what an

FIGURE 2–6.   *Moving from Content Standard to Performance Indicators*

Content standard: Problem solving

One performance standard expressing what is meant by problem solving:
The ability to find patterns among certain types of problems

Indicators of this performance standard that I can observe in student behavior:

beginning ability: treats all problems alike, does not recognize patterns

developing ability: recognizes differences among problem types, but is not consistent in doing so

competent performance: recognizes differences among problem types and consistently applies different problem solving strategies to appropriate problem types

ability will look like in the context of student work, but they must also reflect what you are able to integrate into your mathematics lessons. In other words, you need to give students opportunities to practice the abilities you are identifying. In addition, remember that performance standards and performance indicators are guides to help you and your students make connections between daily mathematics lessons and their understanding the whole of mathematics. Both can be revised as you receive feedback through student work.

How will identifying performance standards affect my teaching?

The heart and soul of alternative assessment is to alert students, parents, administrators, and the community at large to the criteria that shape assessment tasks and provide the basis for judging performance. Making public the criteria against which students will be judged is radically new: we once believed that doing so would promote "teaching to the test." We have since realized that if we want to increase the literacy level of our students, everyone has to be involved in helping students practice skills like reasoning, representing and organizing data, communicating about mathematics, and applying number sense. The teaching-learning process has become more collaborative.

The original meaning of *assess* was "to sit down beside" (from the Latin *as + sidere*). It has come to mean careful judgment, the kind of evaluation you can achieve only when "sitting down beside." Sitting down beside suggests new roles for the teacher and student, roles that have emerged because teacher and student know what important abilities they both will observe and comment on.

The purposes of learning are also very different from what was once believed. In the past, schooling was driven by the desire "to pass down" a certain level of information viewed as requisite to being a literate person. Today, the task is to provide students with learning skills that will prepare them for a world in which information is more complex and symbolic, changes rapidly, increases exponentially, and is often provided through technology. Likewise, our understanding of how learning occurs has changed dramatically. In the past, rote memorization was the primary learning strategy. Presently, research evidence supports active learning strategies in which children are given opportunities to construct understanding in contexts that make sense to them. In the current view of education, where learning, not testing, is at the heart of the classroom experience, students must understand what is occurring as instruction unfolds. The call to make school more lifelike requires that we design our lessons so that students apply mathematics, not memorize procedures, that they learn to pose and solve problems rather than compute problems with predefined solutions.

As you are clearer about the mathematics abilities you want your students to succeed at and the performance indicators that will help both you and them describe how they are learning these abilities, you will find ways to model and communicate these abilities to your students. They will become an explicit part of your everyday classroom life, much as an Olympic diver brings to her everyday practice the knowledge of what dives or techniques need to be refined. Because she has been through a series of performance-based competitions, this diver does not depend solely on her coach to tell her how her performance will be judged. Over time she has gained an intuitive knowledge about her own performance that is invaluable to her as a learner and a performer. As a teacher, you should find yourself less and less in the position of being the sole dispenser of knowledge. Instead, like a coach, you will be an integral part of a learning process that expects a more active role on the part of students, their families, and the larger school community. The assessment of student work will be less separate from instruction; in fact, you will come to depend much more on daily instruction as a way of informing you about the progress your students are making on the larger content standards identified as central to mathematics instruction.

· 3 ·

Creating a Match: Reforming the Curriculum

We just finished the state assessments. They had these open-ended questions on them. My students had never seen anything like these questions before. The kids were a wreck the whole week.

In This Chapter

- ◆ What do I do after I identify performance standards?
- ◆ How does identifying standards and performance indicators help me use new assessment strategies?
- ◆ How do I create open-ended problems?
- ◆ How will creating and using open-ended problems change my teaching?

Key Terms

Convergent thinking involves the ability to select and follow the steps necessary to produce the one correct answer to a problem.

Divergent thinking involves the ability to generate a variety of answers to a problem for which more than one answer may be correct.

Open-ended problems have more than one answer and/or can be solved in a variety of ways. Their "openness" allows a variety of perspectives and can stimulate interest in the communication of mathematical ideas.

What do I do after I identify performance standards?

Imagine that you have identified knowledge of estimation as a content standard you want your students to achieve and have worked with colleagues to articulate some initial performance standards. What happens next? Some teachers believe they need to construct an entirely new curriculum at this point. That task seems too burdensome to many and keeps them from examining alternative assessment in the first place. It is therefore important to realize that using alternate assessment does not mean you have to change everything about your curriculum.

You will, however, probably want to make some changes so that your curriculum will better match your views on assessment and the performance indicators you identify. Focusing on standards and performance indicators will help you make clear choices about the changes you want to make. People are often more comfortable making changes slowly, over a long period. Changes made this way may even be more effective than those made quickly, as they allow for a more thoughtful and thorough analysis. Further, the evolving nature of the change lets students develop their new roles in the assessment process over time as well.

Consider this example: Gena is a second-grade teacher. Last summer her school held four professional development workshops focusing on the identification of content standards and performance indicators for mathematics. During the workshops two standards were developed—estimation and the communication of mathematical ideas. Gena reflects back on these workshops as she thinks in broad terms about the way her students will explore estimation this year. She remembers the discussion with her colleagues about the abilities that "good estimators" demonstrate and the list of performance standards that were generated based on that discussion. (The list is provided in Figure 3–1.)

She wants to be sure she is providing enough opportunities for her students to develop the abilities associated with the estimation performance standards identified during the workshops. As she reads the list she thinks she is providing appropriate learning experiences for many of the items but has to admit that she has never really done much with the use of reference points or compensation techniques. (Using reference points means referring to something known to

FIGURE 3–1.   *Performance Standards for Estimation*

Knows when a given number is an estimate
Recognizes when a ballpark answer is all that is needed
Uses a variety of estimation strategies such as:
> front-end estimation
> compatible numbers
> compensation
> benchmarks
Understands that the level of accuracy required depends on the situation
Senses when an estimate is a reasonable one
Has a sense about numbers in the real world
Understands the magnitude of numbers
Can communicate an estimation strategy
Can talk about sources of estimation errors
Can be flexible with numbers
Has good mental math skills
Uses estimation to check the reasonablesness of an answer

help make an estimate; for example, the average height of a seven-year-old cannot be three feet, because my sister is only four years old and she is already three feet tall. Compensation is the process of adjusting an estimate in order to refine it; for example, I rounded both numbers down, so I'll add 200 to my estimate.)

Gena decides to begin the school year by focusing on using reference points. She looks at the textbook her school has adopted to see how much attention it gives to this aspect of estimation. She examines the estimation file that she has gathered over the years and consults her favorite resource books. She places a Post-it on any page that deals with using reference points to estimate. As she begins to focus on this ability, she realizes that she could alter activities that she has used previously in order to make the use of reference points more explicit. Gena describes the process this way:

> At first I thought I would have to start from scratch. To be honest, I wasn't sure what it meant to use reference points when one of my colleagues first mentioned it. But when I started looking through my files I realized I had estimation activities that could be changed somewhat to emphasize this strategy. Every Halloween I have my class estimate the number of pieces of candy corn in a jar. We would do that again this year, but there would be more explicit attention to the use of reference points. I would follow up with opportunities to repeat the estimation activity once the number of pieces of candy corn in the jar had been counted. The children could guess the number of pieces when the jar was filled to a different level. Then they could estimate the number of pieces in jars of other sizes or the number of objects of a different size in the same jar. These extensions seemed obvious once I focused on the ability I wanted to develop. In fact, I couldn't believe I didn't do more with this activity earlier.
>
> As I thought about the use of reference points, I realized they could be used in other estimation settings as well. In some situations they could help the children estimate sums and differences or interpret the reasonableness of numerical information. I decided that for two weeks I would end the school day with an activity I would call "reference points." I would tell the children a factual statement. Based on that statement, the children would decide on a reasonable number to insert into the second statement. I decided that my first day's statements would be:
>
> There are 21 teachers at our school.
> There are _____ cars in the parking lot.

Gena began with the content standard of estimation and a draft of associated performance standards from the inservice summer sessions. She then decided to focus on one particular ability, the use of reference points. She altered instructional activities in order to highlight this ability. Intuitively Gena had known that providing children with the opportunity to estimate the number of pieces of candy was a worthwhile task, but she discovered that she could expand the activity. Once she focused on the use of reference points, the activity had greater mathematical potential and greater potential for her students to make mathematical connections in everyday contexts. Rather than merely being exposed to opportunities to estimate, her students would learn ways to improve their abilities to make estimates. It was as if the activity had been fine-tuned to provide a clearer picture of the mathematical thinking important to the task.

Once Gena realized that thinking about reference points was improving her instructional planning, her enthusiasm for the task grew and she developed a new activity that she was eager to share with her students. Since these responses are both favorable, it appears as if Gena chose a curriculum task involving an appropriate level of change. The change wasn't so great that she felt over-burdened, but it was enough of a change to make her rethink her instructional patterns and generate new ideas.

After Gena tried these ideas with her students, she could better describe the performance indicators for the "uses reference points" performance standard. She realized that some children could only use a reference point when the jar and the objects were the same but the level of objects in the jar changed. Other students could use reference points even though there were changes in the size of the jar or in the size of the object. A few students could use reference points in all these situations. Through experience, Gena became aware of different developmental levels in using reference points. The developmental model would help her assess future students' ability to use reference points. Through her instructional practice, her ability to assess students' abilities had been expanded; Gena made another link between instruction and assessment.

How does identifying standards and performance indicators help me use new assessment strategies?

Decades back, learning was often viewed as a collection of specific isolated skills (behavioral objectives—see Chapter 2); for example, *subtraction with two two-digit numbers, regrouping from tens to ones*. Often such skills were assessed by way of worksheets or textbook practice pages. Students completed these worksheets or practice pages and handed them in to the teacher, who determined the correctness of each example. An X (made with a red pen, so that it stood out on the page) marked each incorrect example, but the specific nature of the errors was not identified. The X's were merely counted and a grade was placed at the top of the paper. Students were sometimes allowed to use the teacher's edition to correct their own work. They too marked the X's and computed their grades.

The strategies and goals for teaching concepts of whole number operations have changed. Consider the operation of subtraction. Educators still want students to be able to subtract accurately, but they now recommend that students learn subtraction with regrouping and subtraction without regrouping at the same time, rather than learning the two skills in isolation. Further, students are now expected to be able to explain the subtraction process that they use, to apply subtraction skills within a context, and to know when to use paper-and-pencil techniques rather than other methods. Finally, many teachers now believe it is important for children to construct their own subtraction algorithms in order for those algorithms to have meaning.

▶   Before you read further, conduct an experiment. Ask about ten or more adults to complete this subtraction example:

$$\begin{array}{r} 10,000 \\ -347 \\ \hline \end{array}$$

Also note how the people in your sample record the subtraction process.

At least four different recording techniques usually surface during this experiment. Not all the differences are major, but they are observable. Some adults are very aware of the way they were taught to subtract and may make a comment like "Mr. Robinson taught us never to make any marks on the problem." Some adults can't remember whether they subtract the way they were taught, while others admit (sometimes sheepishly) that they do not record the subtraction process the way they were taught to in school. These responses make one wonder why some teachers spend so much time teaching children to subtract in exactly the same way.

Yim is a third-grade teacher who believes that students should construct their own algorithms. She is interested in many more aspects of the children's understanding of whole number operations than whether or not they have arrived at the correct answer. For example, she wants her students to be able to demonstrate that they understand their subtraction algorithms. In thinking about the ways students could demonstrate that understanding, she identifies the following performance standards:

1. Models the subtraction process using base-ten blocks.
2. Develops a system for representing that subtraction process with symbols.
3. Communicates the relationship between the symbols and the materials to others.
4. Understands others' techniques for representing the process.

Having identified performance standards, Yim needs to create activities that will allow her to determine whether they are being achieved. Unlike traditional assessments, these activities are not isolated from the regular instructional patterns of her classroom. She designs learning experiences in which the children, in groups, solve problems that require subtraction. She provides each group with base-ten materials and encourages each student to record the subtraction process in his or her own way. She then asks the students to explain their techniques to a partner.

Yim notes the variety of representations the children adopt. She observes which symbolic methods mirror the manipulations with the materials and which do not. She notices that some children refer to the tens and ones places and some do not. She sees that some children can communicate their techniques to others well and some can only partially describe their techniques. She notices that some children can understand others' methods only when they are similar to their own methods, while other children seem to understand others' methods even if they are quite different from their own. These observations help Yim describe performance indicators for each standard. Yim also decides to observe a similar activity again three weeks from now. It is important that such complex and interrelated ideas be assessed over time.

Let's examine Yim's process. She identified performance standards that in turn determined how she structured her assessment tasks. The ways she devised for her students to demonstrate their understanding meant she could not employ traditional assessments. Her performance indicators required that the students:

- Have materials available,
- Talk to one another, and
- Create their own methods to represent a mathematical process.

When students create their own mathematical representations, their responses are not uniform. Divergent rather than convergent thinking is emphasized. Tasks or problems involving divergent thinking allow children to pursue their own paths and to communicate those paths to others. These tasks are often referred to as open-ended problems or questions.

How do I create more open-ended problems?

Standardized tests are often given in multiple-choice formats. The first way in which open-ended problems are different from those in traditional assessments is that the student is responsible for constructing the answer. But omitting the four or five choices from a traditional problem does not in itself make it open-ended. The problem must be open in other ways as well: there should be more than one way to solve it or more than one answer.

Interest in mathematical problems that have a variety of solutions or solution strategies is growing. The ability to communicate mathematics is one of the NCTM standards. Students are more motivated to communicate mathematical ideas when the problem allows a variety of responses. Interest in open-ended problems has also been generated by concern over how people typically view mathematics. Too many people see the study of mathematics as a search for the one correct answer. Not only is this understanding incorrect, it does not allow for diverse learning styles and can lead to low student interest and morale.

Interest in open-ended problems for instructional purposes carries over into assessment as well. Open-ended problems often require students to explain their thinking and thus allow teachers to gain insights into their learning styles, the "holes" in their understanding, the language they use to describe mathematical ideas, and their interpretations of mathematical situations. When no specific techniques are identified in the problem statement (e.g., use multiplication to . . .), teachers learn which techniques the students choose as useful and get a better picture of their students' mathematical power.

Although interest in these problems continues to grow, the majority of problems presented in curriculum materials are not open-ended. Therefore you may want to create them yourself. It is often helpful to begin with a given problem (the "before" problem, providing the stimulus) and try to make it more open (the "after" problem). As with pictures of the same person as a young and older adult, you recognize that the two problems are related, but the differences between them are often as noticeable as the similarities.

▶ Let's consider some specific problems and how they could be transformed.

Sale!
Dolls $2.52
Puzzles $1.25
Books $0.75
Cars $1.58
Wagons $4.50
How much does it cost to buy one puzzle and two cars?

This type of problem has exactly one answer. It will most likely be assessed as right or wrong. There is little for students to talk about, and the problem reinforces the myth that mathematics is limited to convergent thinking. However, with some minor changes, the problem can be opened up to allow multiple answers that students will want to share:

> Sale!
> Dolls $2.52
> Puzzles $1.25
> Books $0.75
> Cars $1.58
> Wagons $4.50
>
> Imagine that you have $8.00 to spend. Tell what you will buy. Explain how you know that you can afford your choices.

This problem has several answers. Students will be interested in the different ways that others chose to spend the money. The new problem also allows you to learn how students keep track of their expenditures—do they keep an exact total, or do they estimate?

Here is another example. The "before" problem:

> Draw a ring around each rectangle.

The "after" problem:

> You have been hired to write a math dictionary for the students in your school. How would you define a rectangle?

Notice the shift in the mathematical expectations for the students. The original task requires only recognition. The more open task gives students the opportunity to demonstrate what they know about the properties of rectangles. And their answers will give you a much more detailed understanding of what they know and the language they use to communicate their ideas. The sample responses in Figures 3–2, 3–3, 3–4, and 3–5 (all from students in the fourth grade) should give you a sense of the richness of what you can learn about students when more open-ended questions are asked.

There are many similarities and differences in these responses. The properties of the rectangles—the number of sides, the lengths of the sides, and the angle measurements—have been identified although not all the responses include all the properties. It seems clear that some students have a misconception about rectangles. They do not understand that a square meets the definition of a rectangle. Some students provide drawings or real-world examples of rectangular shapes. However, rectangles are not differentiated from three-dimensional shapes that have rectangular faces. Remember, though, that because a student did not provide a real-world example of a rectangle in this task does not mean that she is unable to do so. Also, this task is one of many that could be used

FIGURE 3–2.　*Todd's Definition of a Rectangle*

You have been hired to write a math dictionary for the
students in your school. How would you define a rectangle?

A rectangle has 4 sides. 2 are long
and two are short The long ones
are on the top and bottom
and the Short ones are on
the sides. It has four right
angles

FIGURE 3–3.　*Anna's Definition of a Rectangle*

You have been hired to write a math dictionary for the
students in your school. How would you define a rectangle?

rectangle – a square that has longer sides and
shorter ends. It looks like a square that has been
streached.

FIGURE 3–4.   *Jennifer's Definition of a Rectangle*

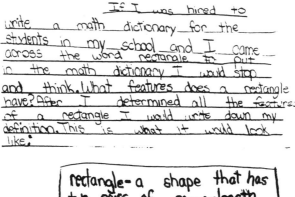

You have been hired to write a math dictionary for the students in your school. How would you define a rectangle?

If I was hired to write a math dictionary for the students in my school and I came across the word rectangle to put in the math dictionary I would stop and think. What features does a rectangle have? After I determined all the features of a rectangle I would write down my definition. This is what it would look like:

rectangle- a shape that has two pairs of same-length sides and every angle is a right angle. It is also a parallelogram.

FIGURE 3–5.   *Jamal's Definition of a Rectangle*

You have been hired to write a math dictionary for the students in your school. How would you define a rectangle?

I have been chosen to define a rectangle. A rectangle is a 4 sided shape. It can be little or big. It is mostly used in math. It can also be used in other subjects. It is very helpful in school. Teachers use it and even the kids use the rectangle in their school. It is shaped like a big book. It also looks like a school. It looks like my schools pizza.

over time to assess a student's understanding of the properties of geometric shapes and their use in the real world.

A teacher may read these responses and decide to involve the students in both the instruction and assessment processes. For example, the teacher asks pairs of students to identify the rectangles in a group of geometric shapes by exchanging definitions and using the definitions they are given to identify the rectangles. Afterward, the partners give each other feedback on the definitions and revise them. A class discussion follows, after which the definitions are revised again. The teacher then compares these definitions with the earlier samples.

Other examples of closed and open problems are provided in Figure 3–6. Now, try to create your own examples of open-ended questions based on ◀

FIGURE 3–6.   *Examples of Closed Versus Open Problems*

Closed	Open
Show a graph about favorite books and ask, "How many people chose biographies as their favorite books?"	Show a graph about favorite books and ask, "What does this graph tell you?"
Show a picture of a rectangle and ask, "What is the area of this figure?"	Ask, "Why would a gardener want to know the area of her garden? What other measurements might she want to know?"
Ask, "What is the value of the 3 in the number 3,472?"	Ask, "Imagine that you had a job numbering the pages in books. Your first book starts on page 1 and ends on page 462. How many times will you write the digit 3?
Say, "Mr. Chang buys 8 plants and one pot. Each plant cost $5 and the pot cost $12. What was the total cost?"	Say, Margo solved a problem. She multiplied two numbers and then added 12 to the product. Write a story problem that Margo could answer using this arithmetic."
Show two towers, one that is 8 cubes high and one that is 4 cubes high. Ask, "How many blocks should you move from this tower to this tower so the towers will be the same height?"	Say, "There are two towers of different heights. They are both built with the same size blocks. Write directions so that someone will know how to decide how many blocks to move so that the towers will be the same height."

the closed problem in Figure 3–7. Think about different ways of opening it up and allowing for more divergent thinking. Try to formulate five different open problems. As you investigate ways to open up this problem, think about how the transformations provide you with different kinds of information about students' mathematical understanding. Use the space provided after the problem to help you organize your work. You may want to brainstorm ideas with a colleague.

How will creating and using open-ended problems change my teaching?

Once teachers begin transforming problems to make them more open, they often become increasingly critical of the problems they typically find in curriculum resource materials. Listen to Michael, a fifth-grade teacher:

> Once I began to think about opening up problems, I couldn't look at a problem without wanting to transform it. I never realized how confining

FIGURE 3–7. *Create Your Own Open Problems*

> **CINEMA SHOWCASE**
> **Now Showing:**
> **THE CLASSROOM BANDITS**
> **All Seats: $2.50**
>
> The feature movie starts at 3:30 PM.
> The feature is 97 minutes long.
> What time does the movie end?
>
> | New Open Problem | Thinking Process and Mathematical Understanding Addressed |
> |---|---|
> | 1. | |
> | 2. | |
> | 3. | |
> | 4. | |
> | 5. | |

most problems were. At first it made me rather angry. Why was my school buying such junk? As I got more involved in the workshop, I started to really enjoy creating my own problems. Since I took the workshop with three colleagues from my school, I have people I can work with on this. We have started an "open-ended problems bank." We all share any problems or resources we can find.

After working with open-ended problems, some teachers begin to think about other ways they are presenting mathematics in a closed manner. They begin to realize there are many ways to limit or control the mathematics curriculum. One teacher said she realized that because of her own bad experiences with mathematics when she was a child, she had been teaching mathematics as a careful, step-by-step process in order to ensure that everyone in her class would be successful. She came to understand that although her students were successful at what she was teaching, she was really restricting their exposure to mathematics. Although her intentions were good, her students were losing the opportunity to develop mathematical power.

Many teachers notice that the way they spend their time changes once they start using open-ended problems. Teachers who have spent a lot of time preparing worksheets to be used over a two- or three-day period find they now only need to prepare one problem. However, they spend much more time reading student responses to this problem than they would have spent correcting the worksheets. Second-grade teacher Shawn noticed this reallocation and began thinking about other uses of his time in teaching mathematics. He realized that he often demonstrated mathematical techniques on the chalkboard. His students were not doing mathematics during this time, he was. Once he was able to let students explore open-ended problems, teaching them techniques as needed, he found his students were spending more time doing mathematical tasks and he was spending less time doing them.

You may want to collect some data about your own mathematics teaching. Monitor yourself for a week. How much time do you spend doing mathematics while your students watch you? How much time are your students doing mathematical tasks while you observe them?

Perhaps the greatest change that takes place once you begin to emphasize open-ended problems is the nature of mathematics in your classroom. It is no longer possible to view mathematics as the search for the one right answer. Further, you spend time thinking about how you will transform closed problems and for what purpose. By addressing these questions, you and your students become clearer about the mathematical abilities you value.

Finally, using open-ended problems will immerse you in assessment. You cannot mark these problems as only correct or incorrect. You will need to find other ways to translate and organize the responses into meaningful data.

· 4 ·

Documenting Student Progress: Descriptive Data

I like the idea of using interviews and observations as part of my assessment program. But how do I keep track of everything I see and hear? How will I ever have time to do all of this?

IN THIS CHAPTER

♦ What are documentation systems and why do I need them?
♦ What ways can I use to document my observations?
♦ How will using documentation systems affect my teaching?

KEY TERMS

A **documentation system** is any tool for organizing anecdotal evidence taken from completed student work or in-class observations that provides an overview of how students are doing on the performance standard or performance indicator being assessed.

Evidence can be thought of as examples obtained from student products or recorded descriptions of student performances that are indicative of student behaviors relative to performance standards and performance indicators.

Descriptive data or **anecdotal data** are narrative rather than numerical documentations of student work. These terms are applied to notes taken while observing a student engaged in a learning task or while reviewing completed student work. The observation or review of student work is done in relation to previously identified assessment criteria and instructional goals that have been shared with the students.

What are documentation systems and why do I need them?

Documentation systems are an essential part of alternative assessment. By documenting student work you create a picture of student growth over time so you can answer such questions as: How is Emily doing? How can I help her become more successful? In general, a documentation system is a tool for organizing evidence obtained from completed student work or observations as it relates to performance standards and content standards identified as important. (See Chapter 2 for a discussion of performance standards and content standards.) Through the organized collection of evidence that reflects curricular goals, teachers obtain a picture of student strengths and weaknesses. Of equal importance, a well-organized documentation system provides all students with a clear idea of what is expected of them and how they are doing relative to those goals.

Standardized test scores give you different information about your students from that obtained by nontraditional assessments. Test scores, or test scores converted to norms or percentiles, tell you the number of right and wrong answers and how well a student did relative to certain kinds of questions. These scores do not tell you what occurred or did not occur during the process of learning mathematics.

Standardized tests are often set apart from what happens in everyday mathematics instruction, and this separation, with its attendant "objectivity," has been perceived as being very valuable. With alternative assessment models, however, the primary goal is to link assessment and instruction so closely that good assessment tasks equal good instructional tasks. In order to link assessment with instruction it is essential to create a documentation system that supports your efforts to record student progress on mathematical curricular goals and that provides feedback to you, your students, and their parents about that progress.

The challenge of course is how to manage information on student performance that comes from more open-ended mathematical problems, in-class observations, journals, portfolios, and group projects or investigations. How can you turn your daily observations of these important sources of data about student learning into something that is both useful and manageable?

Two things can help. One is to identify performance standards and indicators (see Chapter 2). The second is to create documentation strategies. Documentation strategies, performance standards, and performance indicators work together to make clear the close relationship between instruction and assessment. For example, to get the most benefit from observing students working in a group to solve a mathematical problem, you need to be clear ahead of time about what you believe to be important in the process of finding and communicating the solution of that problem. If you design a problem-solving task around specific performance standards, such as the ability to identify, describe, and extend patterns, then the task of deciding what is important in your observation is made easier. Your work is significantly reduced and your students will be clear as well about what is important for them as learners to value and therefore to practice.

One of the perceived obstacles to alternative assessment is managing so much descriptive information. Information about students that is collected over time becomes unwieldy unless you are good at organizing that information. Besides providing a way of storing student products, the organizing system needs to support you in the process of making meaningful observations of students and their work.

Figure 4–1 summarizes the benefits of using a documentation system.

There is no single correct way to document student performance on alternative mathematical assessments. In qualitative documentation systems, descriptive or anecdotal comments provide a clear record of student work; these qualitative comments can also be translated into a numerical score. Any of the modes discussed in this chapter can be used effectively alone, or they can be used in combination. When you are setting up a documentation system, ask yourself:

- Is it manageable?
- Is it compatible with my school's reporting requirements?
- Will it give me the information I need to provide clear feedback to students, parents, and other teachers?
- Can it help me make decisions about ongoing instructional activities?

What ways can I use to document my observations?

The remainder of this chapter focuses on using documentation systems to capture anecdotal or descriptive assessment information from students' completed lessons or projects or from observing students in action. The next chapter concentrates on documentation systems that score or rate student products and tasks. Since reporting requirements relative to student achievement vary widely from district to district and from state to state, a number of models for documenting student assessment data are necessary. Sometimes these models overlap, and the distinctions between them are not always clear-cut. You should change the suggested models to fit your own situation. Don't be afraid to experiment.

Observing students while they are engaged in a lesson

A group of K–3 teachers, working with one of the authors, developed the observation record in Figure 4–2 to help them evaluate student problem-solving performance. They completed a Record of Observation for each child, noting on the appropriate lines behaviors observed in the classroom. When a child successfully met one of the criteria or performance indicators, the teachers placed a check mark next to it. They also jotted down items that needed further practice.

Because these teachers did not want and were not required to translate the descriptive, anecdotal information into numeric scores, they were not concerned about giving a numerical rating. Their goal was to create a descriptive picture

FIGURE 4–1.   *Benefits of a Documentation System*

With a documentation system, you can:
- Develop a picture of student work that is descriptive, not normed, as an alternative to traditional test scores.
- Translate the more complex assessment tasks you are doing in the classroom into data that can be used to report student growth over time.
- Manage information gathered from tasks that are more open-ended.

FIGURE 4–2.   *Problem Solving Record Sheet*

RECORD OF OBSERVATION
Problem Solving in Mathematics, K–3

Activity _____   Date _____

Student Name _____   Grade Level _____

Students will:

1. demonstrate confidence in the process of solving problems by:

_____ volunteering _____

_____ being enthusiastic with purpose _____

_____ communicating with others:

       _____ talking to another group member about the mathematics _____

_____

       _____ talking and listening to the teacher _____

2. illustrate, describe, and model a variety of problems by:

_____ using objects, illustrating with graphs, drawing with pictures _____

_____

_____ repeating the problem in her/his own words _____

3. verify, interpret, and justify solution strategies by:

_____ explaining the problem solving process _____

_____ seeing relationships between problem types and solution strategies _____

_____

_____ checking/testing the "reasonableness" of solutions in appropriate mathematical units

_____

4. construct problems from everyday life with a variety of math concepts by:

_____ forming a mathematics problem and thinking about it _____

_____ telling in her/his own words, forming a mathematics problem in a story, and writing to others

through illustrating, pictures, graphs, and charts _____

_____ understanding how a problem can be solved, understanding the solution strategy _____

_____

---

of a student's growth in relation to the problem-solving indicators. This criterion was used across grades K–3, in an effort to capture a sense of how the students performed over time. The anecdotal information recorded on the documentation sheet provided evidence of student success with each indicator. After using these sheets consistently, teachers could much more easily provide concrete examples of student performance both to students and to their parents during conferences.

Of course, the teachers using this form did not observe each student every day. Instead, whenever a classroom lesson provided an opportunity to practice problem-solving skills, the teacher focused on five or six students, often those in the same group. When group work was the primary mode of classroom instruction, the entire class could be observed in a week, one group each day.

Each child did not have to be observed within the context of the same mathematics lesson because the performance indicators remained constant. In other words, mathematics lessons were constructed with a consistent problem-solving focus, even though the actual content of the lessons might vary. In traditional grading situations, all the students need to do the same activity so that they can be compared on the basis of the content contained in that activity. When your focus is on building abilities that students can transfer to different kinds of learning activities, you do not have to be concerned about holding the learning activity constant. Having the *criteria* as the constants frees you from the pressure to observe all of your students during the same lesson.

There will of course be times when the *content* of a lesson is the focus of your evidence gathering. In those instances, you will need to change to a management strategy that will allow you to collect evidence on the same lesson for every student.

Classroom example: Pacing and measuring   "Pacing and Measuring" is an activity appropriate for a unit on measuring. Elisha describes this activity in her math journal:

> Today for math we played a game called Pacing and Measuring. It was fun! My partner was Tanesha. This is how you play it. One person has to pretended that it is a robot. The other person has to be like a computer and tell the person that is the robot w[h]ere to go and what to do! I found out that Tanesha and I have about the same shoe size but we go different PACES!

Tanesha, Elisha's partner in the game, describes it this way:

> I learned that some people feet are small and big. We didn't play baby steps and giant steps, we played estimating feet and estimating paces. My partner was Elisha. We had to put a ci[r]cle in front of the dierector and the robot do[es] what the director says. We were estimat[ing] our feet and steps. I won, Elisha kind of lost it.

At the end of the activity, the children are asked to draw a map of the paces they took through the classroom.

While the students practice estimating and measuring using the pacing and measuring activity, their teacher observes three pairs of partners. Even though the content emphasis in this lesson is measurement, he uses the problem-solving performance indicators for grades K–3 as a way to observe how his students approach their task. His anecdotal comments about Tanesha during the in-class observations are shown in Figure 4–3. Because the unit on measurement extends over the whole week, he has additional opportunities to observe other students' understanding of measurement and problem solving. He also gets data from the students' math journals.

FIGURE 4–3.   *Observation of Tanesha's Ability to Pace and Measure*

RECORD OF OBSERVATION
Problem Solving in Mathematics, K–3

Activity _Pacing and Measuring_   Date _March 3_

Student Name _Tanesha_   Grade Level _3_

Students will:

1. demonstrate confidence in the process of solving problems by:

___✓___ volunteering   _volunteers to pass out materials_

_____ being enthusiastic with purpose _as lesson begins, chatters with E. — off task_

_____ communicating with others:

    ___✓___ talking to another group member about the mathematics _interacted with E._
    throughout lesson; shares her map with class

    ___✓___ talking and listening to the teacher _quiets JT while I am speaking to class_

2. illustrate, describe, and model a variety of problems by:

___✓___ using objects, illustrating with graphs, drawing with pictures _T + E. drew map_
together of their paces

___?___ repeating the problem in her/his own words _describes map, but has difficulty using_
measurement terms learned in previous lesson — practice on transferring information
* check T's journal entry

3. verify, interpret, and justify solution strategies by:

_____ explaining the problem solving process _____

_____ seeing relationships between problem types and solution strategies _____

___?___ checking/testing the "reasonableness" of solutions in appropriate mathematical units
realized computation error in adding some #s of paces together — initially
thought size foot would predict size g pace — some confusion   * needs additional
work with different models

4. construct problems from everyday life with a variety of math concepts by:

_____ forming a mathematics problem and thinking about it _____

_____ telling in her/his own words, forming a mathematics problem in a story, and writing to others

_____ through illustrating, pictures, graphs, and charts _____

_____ understanding how a problem can be solved, understanding the solution strategy _____

_____

Notice that not all the problem-solving criteria could be applied to the pacing and measuring lesson. Not every performance indicator identified as being part of a broad ability like problem solving is tapped in every lesson. This is okay. Over time you will develop enough variation in your mathematics lessons to provide descriptive data on each performance indicator. And a lesson that does not tap each individual indicator is itself important feedback. The gaps may prompt you to redesign the lesson to capture additional indicators.

Making decisions about redesigning a lesson, you discover the natural relationship between assessment and instruction.

Tanesha's teacher places this Record of Observation in Tanesha's file. On the inside cover of the file is a form on which he enters the date of the observation and makes check marks under the problem-solving criteria in which Tanesha needs more practice. He tries to confer with each student three times during each marking period about his or her progress in problem solving. These conferences are generally held during an individual reading period scheduled each Wednesday for all third-grade classrooms. During this particular school year, the third-grade teachers are focusing only on problem solving as a content standard or an outcome ability for their mathematics lessons. They are discovering, though, that they can use the same problem-solving criteria for other subjects. Next year, they will focus on communications as well as problem solving.

Classroom example: Combinations of nine   Grant's teacher meets with five students in a group. She uses word problems as a problem-solving context in which the children can demonstrate their understanding of numbers. She uses the Record of Observation to document a lesson in which her students practice combinations of nine. Again, the sheet is a tool to capture anecdotal information; her description of Grant's work is shown in Figure 4–4.

As you review Grant's work on combinations of nine, think about the information the completed Record of Observation provides:

- What do these notes tell you about Grant's understanding of combinations of nine?
- Design another lesson for Grant in which he can continue to practice these combinations.

Documenting student work at the completion of a lesson

According to second-grade teacher Diana Murphy, "Sometimes I don't know exactly how or what I want to document until I examine the students' responses. What is helpful to me is to find ways to organize those responses so I can see more clearly where students need more assistance or whether we are ready as a class to work on new material."

Diana gave the open question in Figure 4–5 to her second graders. They had just spent a week exploring bar graphs, so this question served as an informal assessment of how the students were progressing. (The activity could also be used as a pretest before the students begin exploring bar graphs.) The responses of six of her students are shown in Figures 4–6 through 4–11.

Examine each of the six responses and think about what you might learn from it. What is important given what the student has been asked to do (i.e, "Tell all that you know from this graph")? Make notes about things you feel are evidence that the task was accomplished successfully. Also note those things you believe the student still needs to work on. Finally, summarize each student's work in a couple of sentences.

FIGURE 4–4.   *Observation of Grant's Ability with Combinations of Nine*

RECORD OF OBSERVATION
Problem Solving in Mathematics, K–3

Activity __Combinations of 9 (addition)__   Date __April 19__

Student Name _____Grant_____   Grade Level __1__

Students will:

1. demonstrate confidence in the process of solving problems by:

__✓__ volunteering __raises hand to respond to questions   ┼┼┼┼__

_____ being enthusiastic with purpose __Some squirming, arising from enthusiasm as he solves problems__

_____ communicating with others:

_____ talking to another group member about the mathematics _____

_____

__✓__ talking and listening to the teacher __eyes on me__

2. illustrate, describe, and model a variety of problems by:

__✓__ using objects, illustrating with graphs, drawing with pictures __uses counters to model 4+5 and 6+3, treats 8+1 and 1+8 as fact__

__✓__ repeating the problem in her/his own words __can explain counting 4 + 5; describes seeing numbers in his mind despite counters__

3. verify, interpret, and justify solution strategies by:

_____ explaining the problem solving process _____

_____ seeing relationships between problem types and solution strategies _____

_____

__✓__ checking/testing the "reasonableness" of solutions in appropriate mathematical units
__uses counters to check answers/solutions; uses without prompting__

4. construct problems from everyday life with a variety of math concepts by:

__✓__ forming a mathematics problem and thinking about it __makes up word problem: Tanya has 4 cookies, her mother gives her 5 more, how many does she have altogether?__

_____ telling in her/his own words, forming a mathematics problem in a story, and writing to others through illustrating, pictures, graphs, and charts _____

__✓__ understanding how a problem can be solved, understanding the solution strategy _____
__comfortable with counters as means of modeling addition + setting up problems__

FIGURE 4–5. *Family Pet Graph*

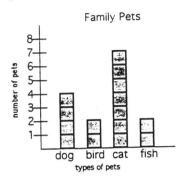

Tell all that you know from this graph.

FIGURE 4–6. *Carolyn's Response*

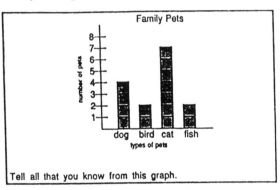

1. I can tel that it is a graf.
2. And theyer is 4 dogs this.
3. And 2 birds.
4. Theyer is 7 cats.
5. A 2 fish.
6. And put them all to geth and you hav 15.
7. And I can tell that they all are famliy Pts.
8. And they is 4 cinds of animls.
9. They are a dog, bird, cat, and fishs.

FIGURE 4–7.　*Frank's Response*

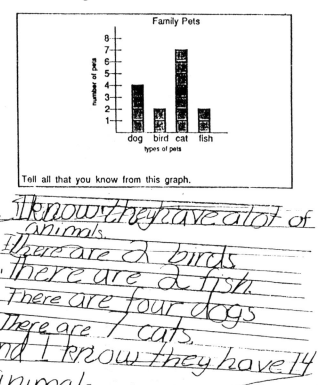

1. I know they have a lot of animals.
2. There are 2 birds.
3. There are 2 fish.
4. There are four dogs
5. There are 7 cats.
6. And I know they have 14 animals
7 there is a big house
8 They must have a lot of litter boxes.

Diana was surprised that many students who she initially thought under-stood the material rather well only mentioned the specific number of each kind of pet or only made comparison statements about these numbers:

> At first I felt disappointed. We had spent so much time reading the graphs for specific numbers and for comparisons. I expected many more of my students to include both types of data in their responses. Then I realized I was getting insights about the types of information individual students focused on. It didn't mean that they couldn't answer questions using other types of information.

Other teachers have noticed how well the context of family pets worked for second graders, even though Frank (Figure 4–7) seems to think all these pets are from the same family! Frank and Carolyn (Figure 4–6) both demonstrate an understanding of how to read a graph, what the *x* axis and the *y* axis mean. Frank has read the number of specific types of pets correctly and yet has trouble

FIGURE 4–8.   *Sofia's Response*

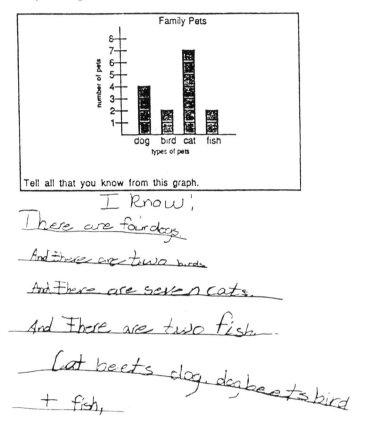

with his computation, stating that altogether there are fourteen instead of fifteen pets.

Frank's incorrect total presents an interesting dilemma: should the inaccuracy be noted? This question can be answered only by the teacher. Diana decided that interpreting graphs, not computation, was the primary focus of this mathematics task, and she therefore did not make notes about computation errors. Diana knew she would have other opportunities to assess computation and felt fine about not doing so in this task. You may want to discuss this issue with one of your colleagues, since it will become more common as teachers begin to make decisions about how to handle more open-ended tasks providing a great deal of student data. The key decision is what portion of the data is important to focus on and document.

Sofia (Figure 4–8) identifies the number of each type of pet, and Diana wants to ask her what she means by "cat beets dog." Diana has a feeling Sofia may have a greater understanding of comparisons than her vocabulary ("beets") suggests.

Diana also wants to talk with Katherine (Figure 4–10) about her understanding of "bigest" and "meadum." While she believes Katherine has provided

FIGURE 4–9.   *Danielle's Response*

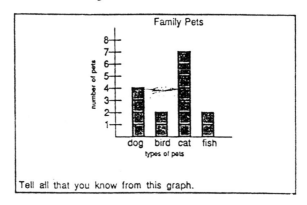

1. There are the same amout of birds and ~~fis~~ fish:
2. There ~~are~~ more cats then dogs.
3. There are four dogs.
4. There are two birds and two fish
5. There are two more dogs than birds and fish.
6. There are three more cats than dogs.
7. There are three less than cats:
8. There are two less than dogs.an

evidence of making comparisons among the pets, she wants to work with her on the vocabulary she uses to express those comparisons.

Figure 4–12 shows the documentation system Diana set up to organize student responses to the family pets graph. By sorting student responses into groups that represent similar ways of thinking about the graph lesson, she was able to create a profile for all the students. Your notes on these six students may reflect observations similar to Diana's or include different information. The comments you make regarding your students' progress are never right or wrong. They reflect your knowledge of your lessons and them. Over time you will develop a sense of the kinds of comments that are of the greatest help to you and to your students.

Likewise, you may have a different way of organizing the interpretation of the student work from this task. Because this interpretation should correspond

FIGURE 4–10.   *Katherine's Response*

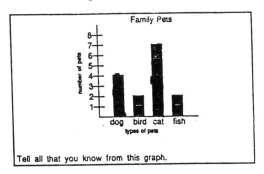

Tell all that you know from this graph.

1. 7 cats, 4 dogs, 2 birds, and 2 fish.
2. No animals are 8.
3. Cats are the biggest number of animals.
4. there 2 birds and 2 fish.
5. birds and fish are the less.
6. Dogs are a meadun # of animals.

to your instructional goals, it makes sense that any system for interpreting student work should correspond to those goals. Therefore, there will be instances when the same mathematics task will be documented in very different ways by different teachers, depending on individual instructional goals. You need to create a documentation system that works for you. It works if it makes it easier to develop a meaningful mathematics profile for each of your students.

More ideas

Finding ways to organize a documentation system can be challenging and may take some testing, refining, and more testing before you are satisfied. We have talked with many teachers about the process of organizing and adapting a documentation system and would like to share some of their comments.

Becky has taught several grade levels and is now teaching kindergarten. She reports that during her first years of teaching she kept a small box with a section of index cards for each student. On these cards she recorded memorable interactions/encounters she had with students throughout the day. She then used these notes when talking with parents or filling out her report cards. Becky reflects:

FIGURE 4–11.   *Tim's Response*

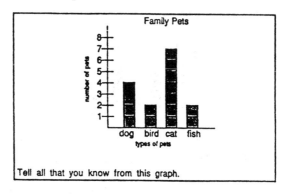

1. The most kind of pet is the cats.
2. The lest is birds and fish
3. The middle is dogs.
4. They are only four kinds of pets.
5. They are four dogs two birds seven cats two fish.
6. They are alot of family pets.

The records I created encapsulated more my reactions to students' behavior and social issues [rather than descriptions of that behavior]. I now realize that I used a combination of evaluation tools, tests, corrected workbooks/worksheets, and these often highly subjective note cards. As the years went on I realized that keeping these notes in a file box was inadequate and more often than not I forgot to write down my thoughts and relied too much on my memory. After a while I organized a three-ring binder, with a divider for each child, and from time to time I forced myself to write observations/notes on each child. What I realize now is that I was always doing this after the fact . . . often at the end of the day when I was tired and certainly forgetful.

A huge shift in my practices came when I began using a form for recording anecdotal student behaviors. On the advice of another teacher, Marie, I now keep a record sheet [see Figure 4–13] on each child on a clipboard that I carry with me throughout the day. I now record what I observe as it is happening or as shortly thereafter as possible. I now have actual quotes of what children say and I can stay on top of their instructional activities. Sometimes, I write reminders to myself on these sheets. I feel my biggest change is that I am now able to record as objectively as possible what I am seeing rather than relying on my memory.

FIGURE 4–12.   *Teacher Documentation of Student Responses*

Name of Student	Code Letter	Descriptive Evidence
Tim	c	appropriate use of most, "lest," middle; can interpret number and types; thinks all pets from 1 family?
Danielle	d	beginning understanding that comparisons go both ways—comparisons relative
Frank	b	1 family??? understands how to read/describe type and number
Carolyn	b	interprets type and number from graph; describes number
Sofia	b?	Cat "beets" dog; dog "beets" bird + fish??? need further conversation
Katherine	c	interprets number and type; need to talk over "bigest" and "meadum"

Code Letters for Description of Student Interpretations of Data:
a.   Is unable to write descriptive statements about the graph
b.   Writes only descriptive statements that tell the number of specific types of pets
c.   Writes descriptive statements that tell the number of specific types of pets and compare types or numbers of pets
d.   Writes descriptive statements that tell and compare the number and types of pets and suggest a deeper understanding of comparisons about the pets

Becky found that because of her chosen documentation method, she could see when she had not written anything about a specific child. As a result, she would plan to interact with that child. Becky also spoke about how hard she is working to record her comments in a manner that tells her what the child *can* do, not what he *cannot* do. By concentrating on student strengths Becky believes her ability to communicate with both students and parents is enhanced.

Another elementary teacher, Geoff, created a different form for recording informal anecdotal notes (Figure 4–14). Geoff uses the form specifically for mathematics and identifies certain mathematical behaviors he believes are important for his students to practice. Like Becky, he keeps a form for each of his students on a clipboard. As much as possible he records his observations on students during their mathematics lessons. He goes over the record sheet with his students, explaining each of the categories to them so that they will not be confused by them. Geoff finds the record sheets an important resource when

FIGURE 4–13.   *Becky's Record Sheet*

Student Mathematical Behaviors

Name_____Week of _____

Monday	Tuesday	Wednesday	Thursday	Friday

he meets with his students, because they provide very concrete examples of what he wants to talk about with them. The sheets also clarify for his students what Geoff values in mathematics.

How will using documentation systems affect my teaching?

Documentation systems allow you to formalize many of the observations you have already been making. You can develop a richer and more complete picture of a child's learning, in contrast to more traditional tests scored by percents and translated into a letter grade. A documentation system helps you focus on broad performance and content standards within your mathematics teaching and better understand what you want your students to learn. Finally, a documentation system is a structured way to manage student information.

As teachers invest in the documentation process they often find they:

- See patterns emerging within a child's learning style that would otherwise have gone unnoticed.
- Diagnose student difficulties better, and can then provide more appropriate learning experiences.
- Communicate better with parents about their child's learning by providing specific anecdotal examples.

FIGURE 4–14.   *Geoff's Record Sheet*

Mathematics Assessment Notes

Student	Questions Asked	Vocabulary Used	Knowledge Demon-strated	Solution Strategies Exhibited	Connections Made	Other

- Find it easier to talk with students about their learning because they can relate it to actual classroom events.
- Find it easier to see the connection between their instruction and student evaluation.

Documenting Student Learning: Numerical Ratings

I was always comfortable grading my students' math papers. I knew whether the answers were right or wrong; it was only a matter of deciding how many points to award to each question. Math papers could be graded quickly and students knew why they received the grades they did. It was always harder for me to grade stories or social studies projects. How do you really know when one project is a B– and another is a C+? I was never sure that someone else would grade the projects the same way as I did. Now they want to change the way that math is assessed. Now I won't be sure about my math grades either.

IN THIS CHAPTER

- How can I score assessment tasks?
- How do I use scoring rubrics?
- How do I create a task-specific scoring rubric?
- How will the use of scoring rubrics affect my teaching?

KEY TERMS

Analytic scoring is a process for assigning a score to a student product. Separate ratings are assigned to different components of the response. The sum of the ratings is the score given to the student's work.

Anchor papers are examples of student work that correspond to a rating scale and can be used as a guide for assigning scores to other examples of student work.

Holistic scoring is a process for assigning a score to a student product in which a single rating is assigned to a student's overall response.

Rubrics provide a way to organize and interpret the evidence from a student product or student performance. They suggest a continuum of performance levels or indicators associated with the ability or task being assessed.

How do I score assessment tasks?

Many of us have concerns similar to those expressed in this chapter epigraph. It is comforting to know that a paper has been assessed fairly and quickly and that peers would arrive at the same judgment. However, you cannot grade a mathematical investigation, a portfolio, or an open-ended question simply by comparing the student's work with the numerical answers provided in a teacher's edition. Does this mean you should never give a numerical rating to students' work?

Thus far, we have described techniques for documenting a student's progress over time using anecdotal records and observation sheets. However, you also can use assessment strategies that result in a numerical rating or score. If you work with other teachers to identify an appropriate assessment task, carefully articulate performance standards for that task, and describe behaviors that indicate different levels of performance within those standards, you'll probably find that your ratings of students' work will be similar. You can embrace the new assessment tasks and still maintain numerical records of students' work. Further, you can be assured that such ratings are obtained fairly.

With a scoring documentation system, you can:

- Assign a rating to indicate the level at which a student product meets predetermined performance standards.
- Translate the more complex assessment tasks you are doing in your classroom into numerical data that can be used to report student growth over time.
- Manage information gathered from open-ended tasks.

Holistic scoring

You may have used holistic scoring to assess your students' writing. You can also use this technique to assess mathematical thinking. In holistic scoring, a numerical rating is assigned based on the work as a whole. One rating is given to the overall effect of the student's response. A simple way to begin using holistic scoring is to sort student papers into three piles: papers that definitely show the student understands and can communicate the mathematical reasoning involved; those that show a moderate understanding and ability to communicate; and those that are inadequate. Then assign the papers a 3, 2, 1 rating respectively. If a great number of papers end up in the middle pile, you can sort that pile into two piles and assign ratings of 4, 3, 2, 1. Or you could sort each of the three piles into two piles, assigning the numbers 6 through 1. Some of you have probably been using similar grading techniques for years, first dividing the papers into three stacks representing high-, middle-, and low-level responses and then recording a check-plus, a check, or a check-minus.

Holistic scoring techniques will be more successful if you have carefully defined the criteria you will use and organized them into a rubric of performance indicators for each possible rating. You can then examine student responses in light of those criteria and assign a numerical rating.

How do I use scoring rubrics?

The California Assessment Program has developed a generic holistic scoring system outlining performance standards for a student's work (see Figure 5–1).

FIGURE 5–1.   *CAP's Generic Holistic Scoring System*

Level	Standard to be Achieved for Performance at Specified Level
6	**Fully achieves the purpose of the task, while insightfully interpreting, extending beyond the task, or raising provocative questions.** Demonstrates an in-depth understanding of concepts and content. Communicates effectively and clearly to various audiences, using dynamic and diverse means.
5	**Accomplishes the purpose of the task.** Shows clear understanding of concepts. Communicates effectively.
4	**Substantially completes purposes of the task.** Displays understanding of major concepts, even though some less important ideas may be missing. Communicates successfully.
3	**Purpose of the task not fully achieved; needs elaboration; some strategies may be ineffectual or not appropriate; assumptions about the purposes may be flawed.** Gaps in conceptual understanding are evident. Limits communication to some important ideas; results may be incomplete or not clearly defined.
2	**Important purposes of the task not achieved; work may need redirection; approach to task may lead away from completion.** Presents fragmented understanding of concepts; results may be incomplete or arguments may be weak. Attempts communication.
1	**Purposes of the task not accomplished.** Shows little evidence of appropriate reasoning. Does not successfully communicate relevant ideas; presents extraneous information.

You can apply the rubric at any grade level and to all types of assessment tasks. Clearly, expectations for effective communication for a student in the fifth grade would be different from those for a first-grade student. However, the rubric provides general examples of the type of factors to consider when assigning a rating.

You will find it beneficial to work with other teachers as you begin to apply holistic scoring rubrics. Looking at students' products together, you can talk about them in relation to the established criteria. Talking with others brings multiple perspectives to the assessment process. Because you and your colleagues represent different backgrounds, cultures, and experiences, you each contribute to the discussion in different ways. These other opinions often help clarify your thinking as well as challenge your own ideas as to how students should demonstrate their knowledge in a specific task.

As a starting point, consider the assessment task in Figure 5–2, which has been adapted from problems appearing in *Seeing Fractions* (Corwin, et al., 1990) and the "Fair Shares" module in *Investigations in Number, Data, and Space* (Tierney and Berle-Carman, 1995). We gave this task to third graders. Each student was provided seven "cookies" that were easy to cut into pieces and to stick on the page. The task was presented orally by the teacher and was written on the task sheet given to each child.

In completing this task, students need to decide what sharing fairly means and then determine how to share fairly when the total number of cookies is not a multiple of the total number of people. The student is asked to model the process using representations of cookies and then to name the number of cookies for each person. Although the idea of dividing fractions or interpreting a remainder as a fraction is not introduced symbolically until the middle grades, a concrete model allows younger children to respond to this task.

FIGURE 5–2.   *TERC Assessment Task*

How can you share 7 cookies fairly among 4 people?

Using the circles (cookies), figure out a way of cutting them to show how you would share them. When you finish cutting, glue the cookie pieces into the spaces below.

Amy's share   Ari's share

Erica's share   Ben's share

Explain your picture:

How many cookies does each person get?   _____

If you know some different ways to write this number, please write them here:

Student responses to this question are shown in Figures 5–3 through 5–7. Examine each response and use the California Assessment Program's rating scale to assign one of the ratings, 1–6, to each sample of work. You may find it easier to make a copy of the students' responses so that you can manipulate the actual pages. We encourage you to ask a colleague to work with you. As you decide in which pile to place a response, try to articulate in writing why you made that choice.

Finding the words to capture your professional judgment is an important step in developing a sense of confidence in the scoring process. For example, if you believe a student's response should receive a 4, write some notes about how that student communicated successfully and how she demonstrated her understanding of major concepts. And remember, you are rating students' responses according to the criteria, not on how they compare with other responses or on what you think the children meant to write. When you have rated the students' responses, compare your ratings and rationales to ours, which follow.

FIGURE 5–3. *Justin's Response*

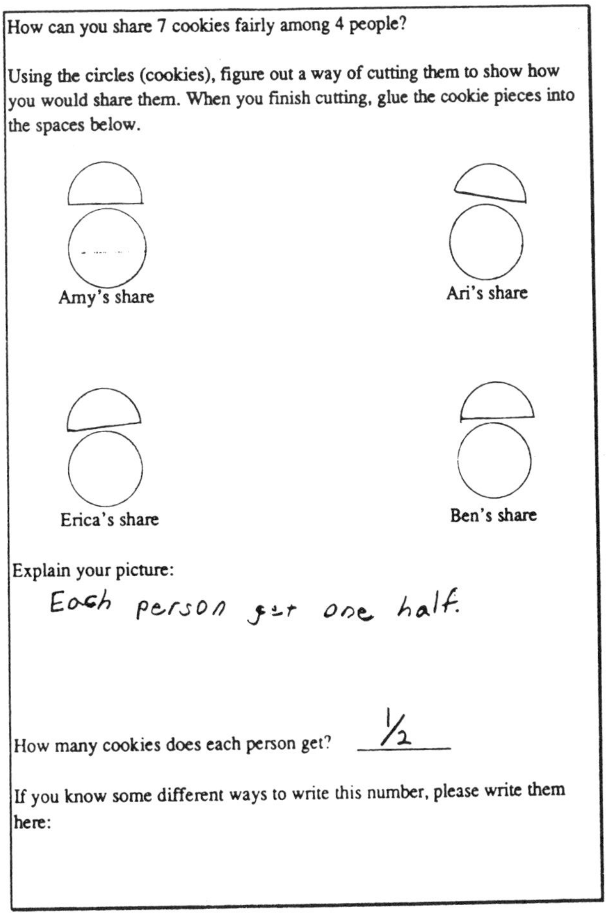

How can you share 7 cookies fairly among 4 people?

Using the circles (cookies), figure out a way of cutting them to show how you would share them. When you finish cutting, glue the cookie pieces into the spaces below.

Amy's share

Ari's share

Erica's share

Ben's share

Explain your picture:

Each person get one half.

How many cookies does each person get? $\frac{1}{2}$

If you know some different ways to write this number, please write them here:

FIGURE 5–4.   *Camille's Response*

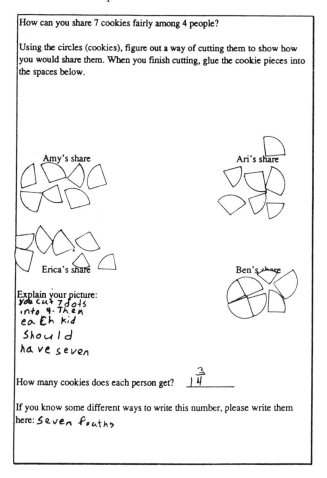

How can you share 7 cookies fairly among 4 people?

Using the circles (cookies), figure out a way of cutting them to show how you would share them. When you finish cutting, glue the cookie pieces into the spaces below.

Amy's share   Ari's share

Erica's share   Ben's share

Explain your picture:
You cu+ 7 dots
into 4. Then
each kid
Should
have seven

How many cookies does each person get? $1\frac{3}{4}$

If you know some different ways to write this number, please write them here: Seven fouths

---

Justin (Figure 5–3): Justin's work is rated a 3. He understands that the cookies can be separated into parts, but limits these parts to wholes and halves. He recognizes that each person should get the same amount but is unable to meet this requirement using all of the cookies. Justin has not fully achieved the purpose of the task and has indicated only the fractional part as the written number of cookies. His work does not need redirection (as in a score of 2), nor has he substantially completed the purpose of the task (as in a score of 4).

Camille (Figure 5–4): Camille's work is rated a 6. Camille fully achieves the purpose of the task. Her technique illustrates the meaning of fraction as division: seven fourths is the same as seven divided by four. For a third-grade student, Camille has found an insightful way to communicate that seven fourths and 1–¾ are different names for the same number.

Olivia (Figure 5–5): Olivia's work is rated a 4. She has substantially accomplished the task. She is able to show the correct physical model and

FIGURE 5–5. *Olivia's Response*

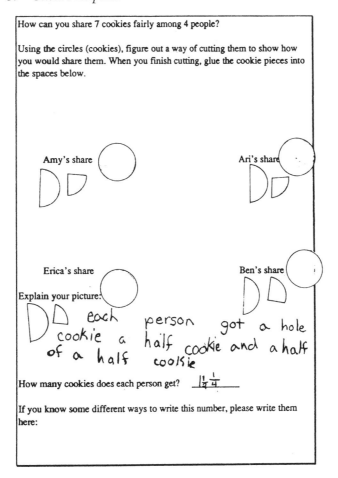

How can you share 7 cookies fairly among 4 people?

Using the circles (cookies), figure out a way of cutting them to show how you would share them. When you finish cutting, glue the cookie pieces into the spaces below.

Amy's share

Ari's share

Erica's share

Ben's share

Explain your picture:

each person got a hole cookie a half cookie and a half of a half coolsie

How many cookies does each person get? _____

If you know some different ways to write this number, please write them here:

to describe the process she used. Olivia has written fractions using words and numbers, but is unable to name the total collection of pieces as one and three fourths.

David (Figure 5–6): David's work is rated a 2. He does not achieve important purposes of the task. He gives each person whole cookies, showing no evidence of understanding that the cookies may be separated into parts. This is demonstrated by his reasoning, "Just give each person one whole cookie." However, he does use all of the cookies, attempts communication, and does not present any extraneous data.

Tiffany (Figure 5–7): Tiffany's work is rated a 5. She accomplishes the purpose of the task. She is able to show a correct physical model and to describe the process she used. She uses word names for whole and half, describes a fourth as "one in 4 little pieces," and identifies the total number of cookies correctly. She does not extend beyond the task (as in a score of 6).

FIGURE 5–6.   *David's Response*

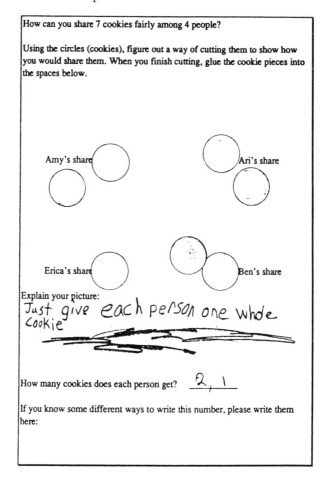

How can you share 7 cookies fairly among 4 people?

Using the circles (cookies), figure out a way of cutting them to show how you would share them. When you finish cutting, glue the cookie pieces into the spaces below.

Amy's share   Ari's share

Erica's share   Ben's share

Explain your picture:

Just give each person one whole cookie

How many cookies does each person get?   2, 1

If you know some different ways to write this number, please write them here:

You may not entirely agree with the numerical ratings we have assigned these papers, but your ratings will probably only differ by one point. That is, you may think that a response that we have rated a 4 is really a 3 or a 5, but it is less likely that you will rate it a 2 or a 6. Such disagreements help all of us fine-tune our sense of the criteria and our professional judgment of a student's performance in relation to the criteria. Don't be concerned if your scores don't agree with ours, as long as you can articulate your reasons for the differences. By articulating your rationale you are better able to ensure that responses with the same features are given the same ratings.

Analytic scoring systems

In analytic systems, points are awarded for particular components of the overall task. You may find it helpful to use analytic scoring when you want to assess skills identified as part of a larger ability such as reasoning, problem solving, or communicating. The overall rating given to a student's work then becomes the sum of the partial scores.

FIGURE 5–7.　*Tiffany's Response*

Randall Charles and his coauthors (1987) have created an analytic scoring scale for problem solving (see Figure 5–8). Use this analytic scale to score second grader Tasha's work, shown in Figure 5–9. (The problem is from the Primary Communications Deck [Greenes et al. 1995].)

We've given Tasha's work a 3. She receives one point for her understanding of the problem. She recognizes that Brenda is standing in line behind five people, making Brenda sixth. However, she does not demonstrate that she understands the term middle, since she puts only three people behind Brenda. She receives two points for planning. Identifying the people in front of Brenda, Brenda, and the people behind Brenda could have led to the correct solution if implemented properly. Tasha receives no points for her answer, because she has not identified the correct number of people and her inability to do so is based on a lack of conceptual understanding. Tasha's rating is 1 + 2 + 0, or 3.

Holistic and analytic scoring systems each have their proponents. Analytic systems provide information about specific strengths and weaknesses, and the separate components of the scale can be weighted differentially. Some educators

FIGURE 5–8.   *Analytic Scoring Scale from* How to Evaluate Progress in Problem Solving *(Charles et al. 1987)*

Understanding the Problem	**0:**	Complete misunderstanding of the problem
	1:	Part of the problem misunderstood or misinterpreted
	2:	Complete understanding of the problem
Planning a Solution	**0:**	No attempt, or totally inappropriate plan
	1:	Partially correct plan based on part of the problem being interpreted correctly
	2:	Plan could have led to a correct solution if implemented properly
Getting an Answer	**0:**	No answer, or wrong answer based on an inappropriate plan.
	1:	Copying error; computational error; partial answer for a problem with multiple answers
	2:	Correct answer and correct label for the answer

FIGURE 5–9.   *Tasha's Solution to the Lunch-line Problem*

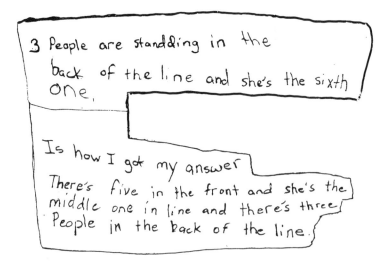

Brenda is standing in line to buy lunch. There are five people standing in front of Brenda. Brenda is in the middle of the line. How many people are standing in the line? Tell how you got your answer.

3 People are standding in the back of the line and she's the sixth one,

Is how I got my answer
There's five in the front and she's the middle one in line and there's three People in the back of the line.

prefer analytic scoring systems because they can help identify components in which a student is weak. For example, a student's work may consistently receive a low subscore in communication. We prefer holistic scoring, however, because it does not divide the task artificially and with it performances can be compared over time more easily. (A student may receive the same total analytic score on two tasks, yet the component scores may differ widely.)

You may prefer one scoring system over the other and may prefer anecdotal data over numerical data or vice versa. You may decide to use checklists and observation forms rather than numerical ratings because you find that anecdotal records allow a level of detail impossible with a numerical system. Conversely, you may find descriptive data overwhelming and feel unsure about how to translate the information into the grades often required by school systems. Your preferences may be hard to recognize until you have experience with both descriptive and numerical data. We encourage you to explore and experiment and not to worry about being right or wrong. Your preferences will become clearer with practice.

Combining numeric ratings with descriptive observations

You can develop assessment recording systems that combine scoring techniques with descriptive records. The teachers in one school we worked with made a concerted effort to add statistics and probability to their third-grade mathematics curriculum. They reviewed the NCTM curriculum and evaluation standards for K–4 and decided to concentrate their curriculum efforts on the collection, representation, and interpretation of data. They worked collaboratively to an-swer the question, What do we expect third-grade students to be able to demon-strate in these areas? and gained a fairly clear understanding of their criteria for these skills. Because their school emphasized numerical grades, they developed an observation sheet (Figure 5–10) and a scoring rubric (Figure 5–11). The teachers first recorded student behaviors appropriate to each skill area. Then, they rated students' performance of the skill as defined for values from 1 through 5. Applying this model, the teachers achieved both goals: they described student behaviors and assigned a numerical value to those descriptions.

How do I create a task-specific scoring rubric?

Although general rubrics are helpful, you can create specific scoring rubrics for specific tasks. Since task-specific rubrics are based on a careful analysis of criteria, using them often leads to more standardized ratings. They also provide more detailed information to the student.

You can create specialized rubrics in several ways. According to Grant Wiggins (1992, p. 30), there are two key questions to consider when creating any scoring system: "What are the most salient characteristics of each level or quality of response?" and "What are the errors that are most justifiable for use in lowering a score?" You may want to ask a colleague to join you in addressing these two questions in relation to a specific assessment task.

FIGURE 5–10.   *Observation Sheet for Data Analysis*

Unit: _____   Dates: Beginning _____
                                 Ending _____

Student: _____

SCORE   ANECDOTAL DESCRIPTION

Skill 1: Collecting Data

_____   Taking surveys _____
                 _____

_____   Formulating questions _____
                 _____

_____   Using resources _____
                 _____

Skill 2: Classifying Information

_____   Sorting information _____
                 _____

_____   Identifying categories _____
                 _____

_____   Deciding what categories are useful to the task _____
                 _____

Skill 3: Representing Information

_____   Translating information (from narrative to symbol or
                 picture) _____
                 _____

_____   Labeling the representations in meaningful ways _____
                 _____

_____   Constructing the representations to display key features of
                 data _____
                 _____

FIGURE 5–11.   *Data Analysis Scoring Rubric*

5	Consistent responses that demonstrate achievement of the skill
4	Some inconsistencies in responses, but demonstrates achievement of the skill a majority of the time
3	Some minor flaws in achievement of the skill prohibit consistent demonstration of the skill part of the time
2	Some serious flaws in achievement of the skill as a result of student misconception which prohibit consistent demonstration of the skill a majority of the time
1	No evidence of achievement of the skill

You can also create a task-specific rubric by adding details to a general ◄ rubric. Consider the following open-ended question:

All-Day Ski Tickets
Adult $18
Child $9
Family $50

The Post family read this sign. Mr. Post said, "I think it would be cheaper for our family to buy individual tickets. His daughter, Maria, thought it would be cheaper for them to buy a family ticket. What do you think the Post family should do? Explain your answer.

Once you have responded to this question to your satisfaction, jot some notes ◄ to yourself about:

- What abilities or skills are needed in order to respond?
- How could those abilities or skills be demonstrated?
- What errors would justify a lower rating?

Some fourth-grade teachers decided to create a specific scoring rubric for this assessment task. They began by working in pairs, discussing the above questions. Then they combined their ideas, summarizing their views in the list shown in Figure 5–12. The numbered items are the abilities or skills these teachers identified; the bulleted items are examples of ways students could demonstrate those abilities; and the asterisked items are ones the teachers thought would lower a score if not met.

Next these teachers examined the general rubric provided in *Mathematics Assessment: Myths, Models, Good Questions, and Practical Suggestions* (Stenmark

FIGURE 5–12. *Beginning Notes for a Scoring Rubric for the Post Family Problem*

1. Understands the information in the problem about family size
   - states that exact family size is not given
   - examples show that there is at least one child and one adult

2. Recognizes the relationship between cost and family size
   - states that there is more than one answer*
   - gives examples of family size that lead to different conclusions
   - makes generalizations about family sizes for which individual and family tickets would be cheaper

3. Uses multiplication (or repeated addition) and addition in solution process
   - shows computation work
   - computes accurately*

4. Communicates solution process
   - organizes data about family size in an organized list or table
   - explanation of thinking is clear
   - gives a mathematical reason for conclusion*

1991, p. 24—see Figure 5–13), which is an adaptation of the rubric used in the California Assessment Program. Working together, the teachers discussed how details could be added to this general rubric to make it task specific. Their earlier notes were very helpful.

After they had created a working model, the teachers assigned the problem to more than sixty students. Based on the results, they made some adjustments: for example, they added another level, since they identified five distinct levels in children's answers to this problem. However, it is important to establish a working draft of the criteria before assigning the assessment task, since you want to be sure you are establishing your own criteria, not merely treating your class as a "normal" population. The final rubric for the problem is shown in Figure 5–14.

Figures 5–15 through 5–19 are five fourth graders' responses to this question, one for each level identified in the rubric. If you try this assessment task with fourth graders, you can use these samples as anchor papers as you score their work.

It will not be possible for you to create such a detailed numerical rating system for every task. Just remember that identifying criteria is the important

FIGURE 5–13.   *General Scoring Rubric from* Mathematics Assessment *(Stenmark 1991)*

Top Level
- Contains a complete response with clear, coherent, unambiguous, and elegant explanation
- Includes clear and simple diagram
- Communicates effectively to an identified audience
- Shows understanding of the question's mathematical ideas and processes
- Identifies all the important elements of the question
- Includes examples and counter examples
- Gives strong supporting arguments
- Goes beyond the requirements of the problem

Second Level
- Contains a good solid response with some of the characteristics above, but probably not all
- Explains less elegantly, less completely
- Does not go beyond requirements of the problems

Third Level
- Contains a complete response, but the explanation may be muddled
- Presents arguments but incomplete
- Includes diagrams but inappropriate or unclear
- Indicates understanding of mathematical ideas, but not expressed clearly

Fourth Level
- Omits significant parts or all of the question and response
- Has major errors
- Uses inappropriate strategies

FIGURE 5–14.   *Final Scoring Rubric for the Post Family Problem*

Top Level
- Contains a complete response with clear, coherent and unambiguous explanation
- Recognizes that the family membership determines which tickets should be bought
- Provides an example of Post family membership for which the family ticket would be cheaper and provides an example of membership for which individual tickets would be cheaper
- Provides some generalizations such as "if there are two adults and more than one child it will always be cheaper to buy the family ticket" to describe possibilities, or provides a table or chart with a listing of the options

Second Level
- Contains a good solid response with some of the characteristics above, but probably not all
- Provides one possible model for the Post family and accurately determines which method of buying tickets would be cheaper
- Makes some attempt to consider other cases or recognizes that family membership determines the answer

Third Level
- Contains a good solid response with some of the characteristics above, but probably not all
- Provides one possible model for the Post family and accurately determines which method of buying tickets would be cheaper
- No other models for the family are considered

Fourth Level
- Identifies which method would be cheaper, but family model disagrees with data in problem, or computation is inaccurate or enough explanation is not provided
- States that more information is needed, but does not give an example

Fifth Level
- Omits significant parts or all of the question and response
- Has major errors
- Uses a nonmathematical justification such as "families should buy family tickets" or "they should do what the father says"

thing. Doing so allows you to assign ratings to student work by comparing that work with the criteria, rather than by comparing one student's work with another's.

You can also use the list of performance indicators in Figure 5–12 as a basis for descriptions of high-, middle- and low-level responses. For example

- A high-level response explains that whether individual tickets or a family ticket is cheaper depends on family size. Examples for both conclusions are given and some generalizations are made. Accurate computations are included.

FIGURE 5–15.   *Top-Level Response*

Solve this problem.
Give a complete an answer as possible.
Explain your thinking.

All Day Tickets	
Adult	$18
Child	$9
Family	$50

The Post family read this sign. Mr. Post said,
"I think it would be cheaper for our family
to buy individual adult and child tickets."
His daughter, Maria, thought it would be
cheaper for them to buy a family ticket.
What do you think the Post family should do?

I think the Post Family should find
out the cost of 3 individual tickets or
then the price of family tickets;

Individual   Family

        18                    $50
        18
   $ 45

The family should buy individual
tickets if there are 2 adults and
less than 2 children. If there are
any more people the family should buy
a family ticket because it is only
$50. This problem does not tell how
many people there are in the family so
there is more than one solution.

- A middle-level response identifies one possible family configuaration and accurately computes the cheaper method for that family. There may be some recognition that other answers are possible, but this idea is not pursued. A reasonable written explanation is given.
- A low-level response gives only a superficial answer to the question, or identifies one possible family configuration but includes inaccurate computations or does not match the information given. There is little or no written explanation.

You can then assign the numerical ratings 3, 2, 1 to responses that are similar to these descriptions.

You can also create a task-specific analytic scoring rubric. Imagine that you have assigned second or third graders this task (adapted from Greenes et al. 1995):

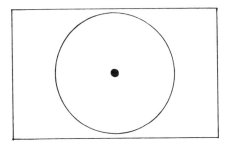

What is your favorite time of day?
Write the time.
Tell why it is your favorite.
Draw a clock face to show the time.

What would you expect the students to demonstrate? Again, take a few minutes to collect your thoughts. You could decide to identify a few skills or abilities needed to perform the task and then create a scale for each of them. An example is provided in Figure 5–20.

FIGURE 5–16. *Second-Level Response*

Solve this problem.
Give a complete an answer as possible.
Explain your thinking.

All Day Tickets
Adult $18
Child $9
Family $50

The Post family read this sign. Mr. Post said, "I think it would be cheaper for our family to buy individual adult and child tickets." His daughter, Maria, thought it would be cheaper for them to buy a family ticket. What do you think the Post family should do?

It is not posable beacuse
1. How many peaple are in the family.
2. How much muny do they have.
3. Do they have Difrent prices at Difrent times

If fit is only the Farther Daughter and Mother
1. It would be cheeper
2. If they buy inoaviul tickets cost=$50

FIGURE 5–17.   *Third-Level Response*

Solve this problem.
Give a complete an answer as possible.
Explain your thinking.

All Day Tickets		The Post family read this sign. Mr. Post said, "I think it would be cheaper for our family to buy individual adult and child tickets." His daughter, Maria, thought it would be cheaper for them to buy a family ticket. What do you think the Post family should do?
Adult	$18	
Child	$9	
Family	$50	

Father 18
way 18
+ 9
45 $

Marias
way   50$

I think they should buy a individual tickets because it is cheaper It is only 45 dolloers for individual tickets and 50 for family tickets!

1 child   9$
2 adults 16$

FIGURE 5–18.   *Fourth-Level Response*

Solve this problem.
Give a complete an answer as possible.
Explain your thinking.

All Day Tickets		The Post family read this sign. Mr. Post said, "I think it would be cheaper for our family to buy individual adult and child tickets." His daughter, Maria, thought it would be cheaper for them to buy a family ticket. What do you think the Post family should do?
Adult	$18	
Child	$9	
Family	$50	

I think The post family should buy Individual Tickets. Because It is to mush to buy famly tickets

18.00
9.00
50.00
77.00

FIGURE 5–19.   *Fifth-Level Response*

Solve this problem.
Give a complete an answer as possible.
Explain your thinking.

All Day Tickets	
Adult	$18
Child	$9
Family	$50

The Post family read this sign. Mr. Post said.
"I think it would be cheaper for our family
to buy individual adult and child tickets."
His daughter, Maria, thought it would be
cheaper for them to buy a family ticket.
What do you think the Post family should do?

> I think they should do it
> individual or if they hate
> anuf money they coud
> go pay family.

> They can do it eney
> way if they have anuf
> money

FIGURE 5–20.   *Analytic Scoring Guide for the Favorite Time Problem*

Times Match
0 Written description, written time, and time shown on clock are each different
1 Two of the three times correspond
2 All three of the times correspond

Clock Representation
0 There is no attempt or totally inappropriate attempt
1 Clock is partially correct, but contains some flaws
2 Recording of numerals, position of numerals, and lengths of hands are correct

Written Representation
0 There is no attempt or totally inappropriate attempt
1 It is partially correct, but contains some flaws
2 Numbers and colon are written correctly or time is written in words correctly

Finally, you can have your students help create the criteria for an assessment task. When students participate, they feel more ownership of the criteria. Although students cannot suggest detailed descriptions until after a problem is solved, they can provide general criteria: "organizes information in a table or graph" or "computes accurately." When criteria are clear, students can rate their own (self-assessment) or another student's work. Empowering students in this way may help decrease the learned helplessness some students experience with regard to mathematics.

How will using scoring rubrics affect my teaching?

Using scoring rubrics offers you wonderful opportunities for personal professional development. Through them you can

- Engage in exhilarating discussions with your peers.
- Change your students' attitudes about their role in the learning process.
- Provide further focus to your curriculum goals.
- Gain a broader and deeper understanding of your students' abilities.

One of the strengths of this model of assessment is that it allows you to gain a richer understanding of what students know and how they think. You will also gain confidence in your professional judgments because they will be based on clearer criteria and you will have collected evidence that demonstrates how and when those criteria were met. This richer picture stands in contrast to more traditional tests, which are scored by percents and translated into letter grades. By using scoring rubrics you are emphasizing the articulation of performance criteria within the teaching and learning process while at the same time gathering data that can help you give feedback to the student, the student's parents, the school, your community, and the educational community at large.

· 6 ·

Interviews and Group Assessments

*This year I've started what I call
"Special Time" with my students.
About every two months I schedule an
interview with each student. The
children look forward to it and so do I.*

IN THIS CHAPTER

* Why is it important to have multiple sources of information?
* How can I use diagnostic interviews in my classroom?
* How can I assess students in cooperative learning groups?
* How will the use of multiple sources of evidence strengthen my teaching?

KEY TERMS

Clinical interviews were used originally in clinical settings to research students' thinking. In mathematical classrooms they can provide students with opportunities to model and explain their understanding of mathematical concepts. A script, or protocol, is sometimes used to ensure that interviews of all students follow a similar structure.

Cooperative learning groups are small groups of students working together. The emphasis in this collaboration is on students communicating their ideas in order to help one another learn.

Cooperative problem solving is a specific example of cooperative learning. This term is sometimes used when the group is focusing on a problem-solving task.

Diagnostic interview is a synonym for clinical interview. Since the word *diagnostic* emphasizes the assessment nature of the process, diagnostic interview is used in this chapter.

Protocols define the interview conditions and possible questions. A script may be provided and rules of interaction established so that interview conditions will be similar regardless of the particular interviewer or interviewee.

Project-based instruction focuses on activities that usually last longer than one lesson and often involve more than one subject. Students may work independently or in small groups, and the project often evolves as student interest is defined.

Validity is an essential component of assessment tasks. The tasks must assess what they purport to assess and reflect the kinds of instructional tasks with which the student is familiar. Inferences that assessors make must be supported through multiple sources of evidence across assessment tasks.

Why is it important to have multiple sources of information?

By using multiple sources of information, you get a clearer picture of your students' understanding of mathematics. You are able to make your assessment practices more equitable and to increase the likelihood that the generalizations you make are valid.

As mentioned in Chapter 1, there is increased interest in using multiple assessment strategies to ensure that all students have the opportunity to demonstrate their understanding of mathematics. By using a variety of assessment tasks, you minimize the bias of a particular performance format. For example, if written responses to open-ended problems are your only source of data, students who have difficulty writing are not able to demonstrate their understanding. Using varying contexts is another way to make sure that your assessment tasks are accessible to all students. Probability examples given within the context of a deck of cards are not meaningful to someone who is not familiar with playing cards. Providing students a variety of ways to demonstrate what they know about mathematics and a variety of contexts in which to apply mathematical ideas supports equitable assessment practices in your classroom.

Using multiple sources of evidence also helps you make valid inferences. If a student misuses a mathematical term once, she may be just being careless. However, if she misuses the term in the same way a number of times, you can be reasonably confident she has a misconception about that term. Inconsistent responses give you information as well. For example, consider these two pieces of data about Timothy:

- He is able to write the numbers 11 through 99 and to use base-ten blocks to represent those numbers.
- When given a word problem that requires him to find the sum of 12 and 21, he uses unit counters to represent the numbers and solves the problem correctly.

The two facts tell you that Timothy is able to represent numbers in tens and ones, but does not necessarily do so in all situations. Knowing just one fact or the other might very well lead you to an incorrect conclusion.

Minimizing bias and using multiple sources of evidence helps ensure validity. Validity is also supported when assessments involve the same instructional strategies you use in your mathematics classes every day. Most likely, working with students one-on-one and having students work in groups are two common instructional formats in your classroom. As such, they should be incorporated into your assessment strategies as well.

How can I use diagnostic interviews in my classroom?

Teachers know how important it is to work with students one-on-one. Instructional breakthroughs often happen when teachers interact with students this way. Diagnostic interviews are one-on-one interactions that focus on assessment. Although these interviews are time-consuming, they are well worth the investment. Through diagnostic interviews with your students, you can:

- Gain insights into their conceptual understanding and reasoning.
- Identify their misconceptions or lack of connection.
- Discover their attitudes toward mathematics.
- Assess their ability to communicate their mathematical ideas.

Interviews give your students opportunities to demonstrate their understanding of particular concepts, and through them you communicate to your students that you value their thinking. You will find they look forward to talking with you about what they are learning. Some interviews follow a formal protocol, while others are more open—more like a conference. In either case, you are able to mold your questions based on student responses. This flexibility often allows you to gain information you wouldn't obtain from a different assessment strategy.

Diagnostic interviews require specific classroom management skills. Your class needs to understand the purpose of the interviews and how you expect them to behave. The rest of your students will need to work independently when you are working with an individual child or a small group of children. Further, it is best if they are engaged in instructional activities that encourage conversations. Students being interviewed may be very self-conscious in a silent classroom. You may want to ask parent or community volunteers to work with small groups while you are conducting interviews. Since diagnostic interviews serve a specific purpose, you will want to designate a specific place for them. Some teachers create a "private place" in a corner of their classroom.

Once behavior, time, and place have been established, you need to prepare for the interview. (An interview may involve one student or two or three students, but it's best to hold individual interviews when you're just beginning to use this technique. Although group interviews allow you to interview more students in less time, they can be more difficult to draw inferences from and to record.) First, you need to designate a problem, task, or series of questions around which to focus the interview. To do so, you need to reflect on what you want to learn about your students' thinking.

It helps to identify a big idea, then think about how students could demonstrate knowledge of that big idea—in other words, determine performance standards. For example, if you were planning to interview fourth graders about measurement, you might create opportunities for them to demonstrate their ability to:

- Understand attributes—length, area, volume, weight, and so on—that can be measured.
- Associate the appropriate tools and units for measuring the different attributes.
- Estimate and measure within a reasonable margin of error.

Identifying these standards will help you construct your interview. Given the list above, you might start the interview by showing the student a copy of a book and asking, What could you measure about this? As the student identifies attributes, you might proceed, How could you measure that? or What would you estimate the length [or whatever] of this book to be?

Let's consider an example. Jacob, a first-grade teacher, wanted to learn more about his students' counting ability, in particular the counting strategies they used when solving problems. First he made a list of counting strategies his students had been exploring in their mathematics activities:

- Set recognition.
- Counting by ones.
- Skip counting.
- Counting on.
- Counting back.

Then he devised a series of tasks that he thought would provide him with information about the strategies. He didn't want the interview to be too complex, so he didn't include opportunities for students to demonstrate all the strategies.

Here is a transcription of an interview he had with one of his students:

JACOB: Nadia, I am going to tell you a story.

NADIA: Good. I like stories.

JACOB: Do you know what a stable is?

NADIA: That's where horses live.

JACOB: In this story there are eight horses in the stable. The horses are eating hay and drinking water. We'll let this brown piece of paper be the stable. Can you use these toy horses to show me the horses in the stable?

NADIA: Hmm, you said there were eight, right? (*Nadia looks at Jacob for confirmation. Jacob nods*) So, let's see, I need one, two, three, four, five, six, seven, eight. (*She places each horse on the brown piece of paper as she counts*) Okay, here's the horses.

JACOB: Is there another way you could count the horses?

NADIA: I could move them over here. (*She recounts the horses by ones, moving the horses to a new location on the piece of paper*) There's eight.

JACOB: Next the farmer lets four new horses into the stable. Can you show me the new horses?

NADIA: (*Immediately picking up two horses in each hand and placing them on the brown paper*) Here.

JACOB: How many horses do you think are in the stable now?

NADIA: Lots. Let's see. One, two, three, four, five, six, seven, eight, nine, ten, eleven, twelve. (*She moves the horses from one side of the brown sheet of paper to the other as she counts them*)

JACOB: What do you think the horses would like to do next?

NADIA: I think they should go out and play.

JACOB: Okay. We'll have the farmer let the horses out of the stable. How many horses will the farmer have to let out?

NADIA: Need to count. (*Counting each horse as she places it off the brown piece of paper*) One, two, three, four, five, six, seven, eight, nine, ten, eleven, twelve.

Jacob constructed this interview with specific goals in mind. Based on the list of counting strategies he had identified, he created an interview recording form that he used to document the thinking of his students. The form he completed for Nadia is shown in Figure 6–1. Note that he used a check system along with written comments.

Marilyn, another first-grade teacher, interviewed her students to assess their understanding of basic number concepts. Her interview with Mario is transcribed below:

MARILYN: (*Placing six connected Unifix cubes in front of Mario*) Mario, here is a train I built with Unifix cubes. Can you tell me how many cubes are in my train?

MARIO: (*Pointing to the cubes as he counts*) Two, four, six. Six cubes.

MARILYN: Can you make a train that has more cubes than my train?

MARIO: Sure. I'll make a train with eight cubes. (*He connects some cubes and checks the length with the first train*) There's six cubes. (*Counting as he adds the cubes*) Now, seven, eight.

MARILYN: How do you know your train has more cubes?

MARIO: Look, here we both have six. But I have more, seven, eight.

MARILYN: Now I'm going to make another train. (*She removes the six-cube train, makes a ten-cube train, and places this new train directly underneath Mario's train*) Which train has more cubes?

MARIO: (*Pointing to the train that Marilyn has made*) This one.

MARILYN: How many cubes did you use to make your train?

MARIO: Eight.

MARILYN: How many cubes do you think I used to make my train?

MARIO: Well, here would be eight. (*Points to the eighth block in his train and then moves down to the eighth block in Marilyn's train*) So, you used nine, ten cubes.

MARILYN: (*Removing the ten-cube train and placing a six-cube train directly underneath Mario's eight-cube train*) Do you remember how may cubes are in your train?

MARIO: Yup, eight.

MARILYN: How many cubes do you think I used to make my train?

MARIO: Two, four, six. You used six cubes.

MARILYN: (*Removing one of the cubes from the six-cube train*) How many cubes are there in my train now?

MARIO: Two, four, five. Five cubes.

MARILYN: (*Removing one of the cubes from the five-cube train*) How many cubes are there in my train now?

FIGURE 6–1.   *Jacob's Recording Form Documenting Nadia's Counting Strategies*

Student:

✓ Identifies the eight horses correctly
        ___ uses set recognition
        ✓ counts by ones
        ___ skip counts

Organizes counters by moving them from one location to another.

___ Demonstrates another way to count

Repeats the same process, moving the counters to a third location

✓ Identifies the four horses correctly
        ✓ uses set recognition
        ___ counts by ones
        ___ skip counts

✓ Identifies the twelve horses correctly
        ✓ counts all of them
        ___ counts on from eight
        ___ counts on from four

✓ Re-identifies the twelve horses correctly
        ___ without having to count
        ✓ re-counts all of them
        ___ re-counts some of them

Next steps:

- work with skip counting
- ck: conservation of #, memory

MARIO: (*Answering immediately without counting*) Four cubes.
MARILYN: How did you know there are four? You didn't count.
MARIO: I can see four.

Unlike Jacob, Marilyn prefers to summarize what she has learned from a student interview on a five-by-eight card. She keeps a card file on her desk, a section for each student in her class. She completes two interviews with each student every month. According to Marilyn, "I need the notes to help me remember the tasks as well as the skills that were demonstrated. At the end of the year, I have twenty file cards for each student. When I read over the cards, I really get a sense of how much the child has grown during the year. I also find the notes help me identify patterns in the children's thinking."

▶ Before reading Marilyn's notes about the interview, think about what you learned. What do you know about Mario? How would you describe the skills he has demonstrated? How would you describe the skills he has not yet demonstrated? Write your thoughts on a piece of paper. Practice linking assessment to instruction by also identifying any instructional decisions you would make. Now compare your notes with those in Figure 6–2.

Forms and index cards are two ways you can record interview data. You can also use numerical scoring techniques, tape recorders, and video cameras. Some teachers prefer to record the data after the interview rather than during it. However, it is essential that the data be recorded immediately. If you design a recording scheme that allows you to complete most of the record keeping during the interview, you will save a significant amount of time. Also, you will capture student behavior as it is unfolding and thus increase the likelihood that you are representing the student's performance accurately.

You don't need to use the same recording technique for all your interviews. As you become more experienced, you will recognize which techniques works best under which circumstances. For example, you would probably not videotape *all* your interviews, but there may be times when you may want to. A videotape may be the best way to communicate with parents or school administrators or

FIGURE 6–2.   *Marilyn's Notes About Her Interview with Mario*

Child's name: Mario   Date: 10/3

Materials used: Cubes

Notes:

Mario always counted correctly. He counted by twos twice. He made a train with more cubes than a six-cube train by matching the six-cube train and then adding two cubes on. He counted on from an eight-cube train to identify the number of cubes in a 10-cube train. He didn't count backwards on an eight-cube train to identify the number of cubes in the six-cube train. When a cube was taken from the six-cube train he had to count to find that there were five cubes, although he could identify that five was one less than six. He has set recognition of four cubes. Mario demonstrated and understanding of counting on far beyond his ability to use a counting back strategy.

Instructional decisions:

Work with Mario modeling the counting back strategy with blocks and then on using that strategy in a problem setting.

to share an interview with your colleagues. Examining an interview with your peers, you can compare observations, receive feedback on your interview techniques, and work with colleagues to develop a recording scheme.

When you conduct interviews, it is important that students understand their purpose and realize that you will be taking notes. Wait patiently for students to respond. Try to react to the students nonjudgmentally, both in what you say and in your body language. You need to use questions that will probe student thinking:

- Can you use the blocks to model this for me?
- How could you explain this to a friend?
- Why does your method work?
- Is there another way you could do this?

Conducting a series of interviews with the same focus, you will most likely discover a continuum of student performance, with students clustered at different points. As you become better at describing those cluster points, you will find it easier to make instructional decisions and describe the developmental levels associated with them. You will identify the individual strengths of your students on which you want to build. You will see which behaviors have not been demonstrated and perhaps need instructional attention.

Finally, remember that the purpose of the interviews is assessment, to learn about how the students think and what they know. An interview is not the time for instructional intervention. "To assure your credibility for the next interview with the student, it is important not to end the interview by showing the student the 'right way' to solve the problem" (NCTM 1991, p. 29).

Interviews are an excellent way for you to validate students' learning. They offer you individual moments with your students and the opportunity to talk with them about their thinking. However, you will also want to view your students' behavior in groups.

How can I assess students in cooperative learning groups?

In the past, mathematics was too often viewed as an isolated activity. In your own education you may never have been allowed to work with other students in a mathematics class. Fortunately, cooperative learning and group projects are playing a greater role in elementary mathematics classrooms as teachers move from skill-based instruction to a curriculum that values process goals and the application of skills to solve problems. In group investigations, students learn together as they cooperate on tasks requiring them to define problems; gather, organize, and interpret data; draw conclusions; and communicate their results. This mode of instruction lets students experience mathematics as a scientific process and encourages a sense of commitment as they pursue on-going investigations for a week or more.

Although many children now experience group instruction, few participate in group assessment activities. Since it is important to align assessment practices with instructional methods, this disparity needs to end. Most teachers are not used to evaluating group work and express concerns about fairness. Consider these comments, the first from a fifth-grade teacher, the latter from a second-grade teacher:

For the past two years I have been using cooperative learning groups in my classroom. I was really surprised when a colleague suggested that I use group assessment tasks. I remembered when I was in college and had all of these group projects in my education classes. There was always someone who didn't do much work and yet got the same grade as everyone else. It wasn't fair! I wasn't about to do that to my students.

I am trying to use observations in my classroom as a way to collect data about how my students think. Since the children usually work in groups, I observe one group at a time. I try to note both the group process and the understanding of mathematics that is demonstrated. But there is so much going on. I often feel that I am unable to write everything that I want to record.

It is possible to adopt group assessment practices that address these concerns. First, you need to think about your expectations for group work. Teachers who frequently use cooperative learning groups must establish clear expectations for group behavior. Many teachers summarize "the rules" on a list to which both the students and the teacher can refer (see Figure 6–3). The expectations listed make it clear that both individual learning and group work are valued. They also stress the value of communication. These very general guidelines can help you think about how to assess group work. They suggest the importance of group process, individual responsibility, and the group product.

Cooperative learning groups involve more than students sitting in a group. As the name implies, the students are learning as a group in a collaborative manner. Group process is therefore important, as are individual roles within the group. Some proponents of this instructional method advocate assigning specific roles to individuals within the group. For example, one student is the task monitor, making sure the group stays on track; another student summarizes the group's decisions and discussions. Other possible roles include recorder, calculator, questioner, moderator, encourager, strategy checker, and materials manager. Teachers who use assigned roles assess the students according to agreed-on expectations for the role each is assigned: for example, does the encourager cheer on the group as a whole and support individual students who may need encouragement? Some teachers prefer not to assign roles but to let the group members establish their own behaviors.

One way to assess group process is through observation. Recording forms can be simple or complex, whichever best suits your style. The form in Figure

FIGURE 6–3. *Rules for Group Behavior*

1. You explain your ideas.
2. You listen to the ideas of others.
3. You help others.
4. You ask me for help when no one else in group can help you.
5. You are responsible for your own learning.
6. You are responsible for your group's work.

6–4 is used by a teacher who observes a different group of students for fifteen minutes each day. In this case, a group of fifth graders were investigating the amount of space given to ads in a newspaper. Because the teacher notes specific evidence of student behavior, the form captures mathematical thinking well.

Another teacher, who prefers to observe all his groups every day, uses the form in Figure 6–5. He does not restrict his comments in any way, jotting down whatever strikes him as he interacts with the groups, facilitating their work. He reviews his notes at the end of each week, reflecting on his comments and using them to make instructional decisions for the following week.

The first teacher is observing more formally. She has designated both a specific time to observe and specific behaviors for which she is looking. The second teacher's method is somewhat less formal. Some teachers prefer to conduct both kinds of observations.

The nature of group work can vary from working on a problem for one mathematics class to pursuing a project over a longer period. Project-based learning, once extremely rare, is becoming more common in classrooms as educators recognize how important it is to engage students in meaningful contexts in which they can pursue mathematical ideas. Project groups are generally expected to produce some sort of a product—a report, video, poster, scale model. Many teachers struggle with the dilemma of assessing the group as a whole and thus reinforcing the importance of the group versus assessing individuals within the group and thus reinforcing the importance of the individual's responsibility for learning. The tension between these two positions tends to increase as students enter the upper elementary grades and teachers are expected to give letter grades. However, it is possible to structure group experiences so that both individuals and the group are accountable for learning. Here are some

FIGURE 6–4. *Observation Form for Small Student Group*

10/16	Makes Suggestions	Supports Others	Asks Questions
Alicia	Tells group to get data over time as it may be different each day.	Asks Maureen which section she wants	
Sam	Suggests each person work on one section each day.	Tells Alicia she has a good idea.	
Maureen	"We need to decide on the same unit of area."		"Which section do you think has the most?"
Tor	Encourages use of a spreadsheet for recording data	"Maureen's right. If I use pages and you use square inches, it won't work."	"Should we be looking for a percent?"

FIGURE 6–5.   *Observation Form for Several Student Groups*

Date: 11/15   Task: Sandwich Combination

Rani Tim Brianna Caleb	Brianna helped to keep group on task. Group struggled with how to organize data.
Cathy Felix Dillon Kera	Re-recorded data to check that all possibilities were listed. Found two missing in process!
April Fiona Tommy Otis	Good participation of all members. Spent a lot of time discussing problem before listing.
Gina Rosa Wilson Lewis	Wilson participated more than usual. Rosa encouraged group to use a table.
John Julie Sarita Raul	Made connection between this problem and bag of coins problem that we did last week.

examples of instructional strategies that maintain the importance of individual and group development:

- Answers or reports are planned by the group; however, students are called on randomly to present the data and the group is assessed on this presentation. It is hoped that this technique will cause the group to work hard to ensure that each student understands and can communicate the work of the group.
- Groups are given the same assignment. When all groups have reported on their work, individual students reflect on their group's work, telling what they would do the same and what they would do differently.
- Group answers to a problem are assessed and then individual students respond to a problem that is similar to the group problem.
- Individual members of a group are given points for improvement. Since it is assumed that the group helped the individuals improve, the average of these scores becomes the group's score. This technique is designed to

make a student with a weak background as attractive a group member as any other, because such a student could improve greatly.

- Each student submits an individual rating form along with the group report. The form summarizes his or her work within the group. These forms are signed by all group members.
- A group log is kept in which all group work is summarized, including individual roles and contributions.

You may want to try some of these techniques in your classroom. Ultimately, you will probably develop your own methods for ensuring group and individual learning.

How will using multiple sources of evidence strengthen my teaching?

As you offer a greater variety of ways in which your students can demonstrate their knowledge, you are supporting equitable assessment practices. As you increase the variety of data you are able to examine, you increase the likelihood that the inferences you make are valid. As you identify assessment strategies to match each of your instructional strategies, you are further linking instruction and assessment within your classroom.

To make sure you are incorporating appropriate multiple sources of evidence, you need to reflect periodically on whether or not:

- The types of evidence you tend to rely on now provide enough variety.
- The contexts you tend to incorporate into your classroom include contexts to which all of your students can relate.
- Your instructional strategies match your assessment practices.

This focused reflection will increase your professional confidence and help ensure that your assessment practices are fair.

Portfolio Assessment: A Tool for Building Reflective Learners

When setting up a portfolio system, what pieces of work are collected and how do I decide what to pick?

IN THIS CHAPTER

- What are portfolios and what do they contribute to an understanding of a student's learning of mathematics?
- How do I get started with portfolios?
- What should be included in a portfolio?
- How do I evaluate a portfolio?
- What things should I think about in managing the portfolio process?
- How can I use a process folio with a portfolio?
- How can I include students in the portfolio process?
- How can I share portfolios with families and the community?

KEY TERMS

Portfolio implies a collection of materials that is able to be carried, that can move through time with students. In contrast to traditional measures of student evaluation, portfolios can provide a picture of student performance in mathematics over time.

A **process folio** is a folder in which students keep work that falls under designated portfolio categories. This collection of work provides students with an opportunity to include their best pieces in each category.

What are portfolios and what do they contribute to an understanding of a student's learning of mathematics?

In keeping with its Latin roots, the term *portfolio* implies a collection of materials that are transportable, that will follow students through time. Because portfolios document students' abilities over time, they can provide a longitudinal and developmental picture of students that is distinctive from traditional measures of mathematical performance. However, putting student material between the covers of a folder is not in and of itself portfolio assessment.

For the portfolio process to be meaningful to your students and to you as a teacher, it should exhibit three characteristics. First, whatever mathematical work is collected should be purposeful, with selections or entries chosen based on predetermined categories. Second, as with every assessment strategy, the criteria or performance indicators used to evaluate a portfolio must address the performance standards you have identified as important to your mathematics program. Third, portfolios should be used as a natural part of your instructional and assessment process, not as an extra enrichment activity with no direct impact on your everyday mathematics program.

▶ Portfolios are an enticing yet sometimes difficult means of nontraditional evaluation for teachers to carry out in their classrooms in a way that links assessment with instruction. If you are considering using a portfolio process as part of your mathematics program, you might begin by thinking about the questions listed below. Jot down some thoughts next to each one as a way to identify your own ideas before reading further:

- What role do you envision your students will have in the portfolio process?
- In what ways do you think portfolios will contribute to your students' understanding of mathematics?
- As a teacher, what do you hope to gain from a portfolio process?
- How will you link portfolios with your classroom instruction?
- How do you plan to evaluate a portfolio?
- What will you do with the results of your evaluation?
- How will you manage issues like storage, organization, and production?

One of the most important contributions inherent in using portfolios is the opportunity you and your colleagues have to discuss two ideas central to linking assessment with instruction: what you value in mathematics and what you believe your students should learn in mathematics. These discussions help you decide what you want to emphasize in your mathematics lessons.

Teachers frustrated by the narrow, skill-dominated paper-and-pencil tests so long associated with mathematics generally welcome the process of portfolio assessment. Portfolios are a way to emphasize complex tasks that students can perform over weeks and months instead of tasks focused on speed and accuracy. Portfolios also reinforce the idea that not all mathematics needs to be completed in a forty-five-minute class period. In addition, portfolios give your students opportunities to practice their writing skills and their growing ability to communicate their mathematical thinking. Portfolios also support the reality of different learning styles among students. Because most items included in a portfolio are the products of open-ended tasks and student self-assessment is emphasized, a portfolio is a terrific means of individual expression. And because portfolios collect multiple sources of evidence of student learning, they enrich parent-teacher conferences.

Teachers have offered the following reasons for asking their students to compile portfolios:

- To nurture my students and encourage them to have a positive self-concept about mathematics.
- To help me change the way I teach mathematics.
- To help me integrate the NCTM standards into my classroom.
- To put students in charge of their own mathematical learning.
- To give me a tool for communicating with parents.
- To encourage students to link mathematics with other subjects.
- To help accommodate the diversity of learning styles I have in my classroom.
- To document student development in mathematics.

How do I get started with portfolios?

Starting a portfolio process is a difficult task to do alone. It is hard to be clear about the reasons for having portfolios as part of your mathematics program and how to fit a portfolio process into your existing program. Like many of the other aspects of nontraditional assessment, the process becomes easier when another colleague is involved. We'd like to share the experience of Patty, Sylvia, and Marsha, three third-grade teachers in the same school building who decided to begin a portfolio program in mathematics.

These teachers had attended two inservice sessions on portfolio assessment offered by their local education service agency at the end of the previous school year. After the sessions, they were eager to try to integrate portfolios into their mathematics classes. Each had some familiarity with the NCTM standards but had been at a loss about how to make them a part of their everyday mathematics teaching. They felt portfolios might be a way to do just that.

In August, before classes began, they took advantage of time set aside for grade-level planning and brainstormed what their portfolio program would do. They started by discussing what they wanted to emphasize in their mathematics teaching, a way of beginning suggested at the inservice sessions. There was instantaneous agreement that portfolios would be a wonderful tool to promote more written and oral communication about mathematics.

Patty and Sylvia had students keep journals in language arts; Sylvia had her students keep a mathematics journal as well. Each was impressed by how the journals promoted student reflection. Sylvia set aside time for students to write about their mathematics lessons and always provided a focusing question— What do you think was important about the mathematics lessons we have been working on this week? or What role did you play in your group to complete your mathematics lesson? Sylvia and Patty saw the step from journals to portfolios as very logical.

As the discussion continued, someone suggested mathematical connections as another area in which portfolios could play an important role. All three teachers thought that if portfolios encouraged student to see connections between mathematics and other subjects as well as connections among mathematical topics, they would be an important addition to their mathematics program. Because they were concerned about how they would manage the portfolio process, the opportunity the portfolio provided to document student progress in other subject areas seemed quite important.

Marsha was concerned that they were not addressing any specific content and felt they should emphasize mathematical concepts. After some debate, they decided to focus on patterns and relationships, which is one of the NCTM standards for kindergarten through fourth grade. However, Sylvia was not convinced this was the best choice. She believed an understanding of whole number computation would be a better focus, because a number of children still had computation problems in the third grade.

Nevertheless, at the end of their first meeting, Sylvia, Marsha, and Patty agreed that these three areas—written and oral communication about mathematics, mathematical connections, and patterns and relationships—gave them enough direction to begin the portfolio process.

The next step was to talk about what student work related to the three areas of emphasis to include in the portfolio. However, the teachers soon discovered they could not decide what kind of student products they wanted in the portfolio without establishing the portfolio's purpose. Why did they want to undertake mathematics portfolios? What did they believe a portfolio would tell them about their students that traditional tests would not? They had decided what they wanted to emphasize but were unclear why portfolios were the best strategy for doing so.

Marsha wanted to try portfolios because she felt they would involve her students more directly in learning mathematics. She had just returned to teaching third grade after teaching fifth grade for three years. She had been concerned about how afraid her fifth graders were of mathematics; many, especially the girls, seemed unable to learn because they were so afraid of not getting the right answer, of making mistakes. She hoped that giving younger students an opportunity to work on tasks that did not always require a single answer would give them more confidence in their mathematics ability by the time they reached upper elementary and middle school. They might also begin to see mathematics as something other than getting one right answer.

Though Sylvia and Patty had not taught a grade level beyond third, they also believed that students equated success in mathematics with getting right answers. They all agreed that getting students to see mathematics as something more than right answers was important and that it was equally important for students to take a greater degree of ownership of their learning. They believed that having students make choices about what pieces to include in a portfolio, thus intentionally honoring the processes of reflection and revision, would support their goal of student involvement and, consequently, broaden student understanding of mathematics and build self-confidence.

The three teachers finally articulated three goals for their portfolio program:

- Having students see that mathematics is more than right answers.
- Having students gain self-confidence in their mathematics ability.
- Having students become more active in their mathematics learning.

What should be included in a portfolio?

After precisely identifying why they were introducing portfolios and after establishing mutually agreeable learning goals, our trio returned to their discussion of just what to include in a student portfolio. Sylvia did not want to be overwhelmed with student work, and Patty and Marsha agreed that whatever they decided would be manageable.

The presenter at the inservice session in June had suggested the following model of what to include if you were just getting started:

- A table of contents.
- A letter written by the student addressing the question, From which entry did you learn the most and why?
- A group product, including a letter reflecting on the group process.
- An individual product focused on a selected mathematical concept.
- A revision.
- A "best" piece of work.

This model seemed reasonable and met the manageability criterion.

The teachers knew they would need to find additional time to meet once school started. After considering several possibilities, they agreed to meet twice a week during September, during the time that all the third graders attended a session with a specialist. This would give them a good hour every week.

How do I evaluate a portfolio?

Having decided what the portfolios would contain, the teachers had to identify how the portfolios would be evaluated. These discussions took up most of their September meetings. They drew on what they had learned in the inservice sessions in June. For example, they knew they needed to be clear about what they expected children in the third grade to know about patterns and relationships and about making mathematical connections and what level of communication they could expect from them—in other words, they had to identify standards of performance for their students in each of the three identified areas as a first step in setting up an evaluation process.

Sylvia believed any evaluation system needed to consider the range of student abilities. She also felt that because portfolios stressed development and growth, the evaluation system needed to reflect these attributes too.

Brainstorming about their first area of concentration, mathematical communications, they produced so many ideas about what constituted appropriate communications that they were overwhelmed.

Then Marsha had a suggestion: why didn't they look at some journals a colleague's fourth graders had produced? Perhaps they would be able to identify specific abilities from these samples. Marsha had read about this process in a professional journal, but hadn't had an opportunity to try it. Patty and Sylvia agreed that this seemed to be one way they could organize their work.

Marsha recommended that they sort the journals into three piles, "needs work in expressing ideas," "expresses ideas adequately," and "goes beyond what is expected in expressing ideas." Sorting this way turned out to be difficult. Patty, Marsha, and Sylvia discovered that students really varied in their overall performance in journal writing. Although some students maintained a consistent level of performance across all assigned entries, many others' entries varied greatly in terms of the difficulty the students had with the assignment and the effort they expended. The three teachers decided that a better approach would be to focus on a selection of entries related to the same classroom assignment. Once they did this, they were able to see patterns among children's performance much more easily. Figures 7–1 through 7–7 are entries these fourth graders made when they were asked to write a letter explaining what they had learned in mathematics during the week. As you review them, think about the process Sylvia, Marsha, and Patty were working through.

All these journal entries discuss what the children learned in mathematics during the week. Almost immediately Patty noticed a difference in the language children used. Some of the children had integrated the mathematics vocabulary that was a part of their work and some did not. Other children described what they had done, but not what they had learned. Others described how they felt while doing their mathematics.

Working through this sorting process helped these teachers see what they wanted to emphasize as standards for communication in their third-grade classes. As Marsha, Sylvia, and Patty articulated what made one piece stronger than

FIGURE 7–1. *Tonya's Letter*

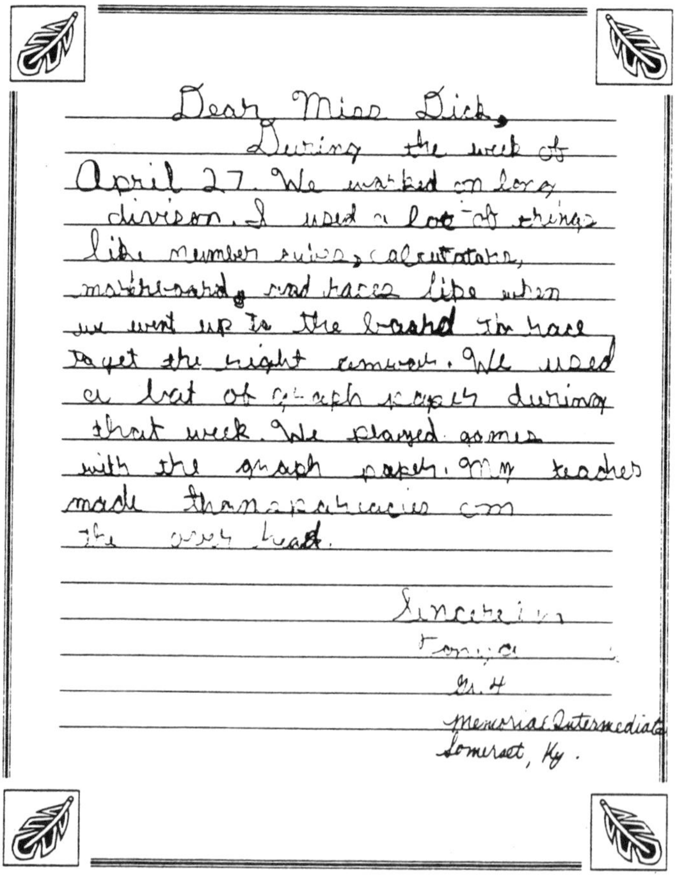
Dear Miss Dick,
During the week of April 27. We worked on long division. I used a lot of things like number lines, calculators, math cards, and races like when we went up to the board to race to get the right answer. We used a lot of graph paper during that week. We played games with the graph paper. My teacher made transparencies on the over head.

Sincerely,
Tonya
Gr. 4
Memorial Intermediate
Somerset, Ky.

FIGURE 7–2. *Brett's Letter*

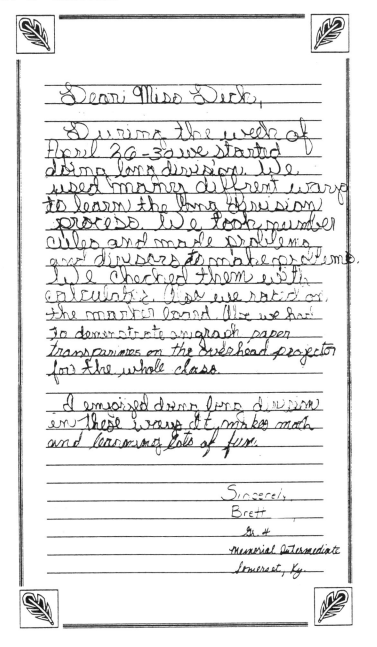

another, they found themselves describing things they valued in the students' work. Ultimately they gained a clearer understanding of what they wanted their students to know. Having identified the communications abilities they were looking for, they were able to convey them to their students much more effectively.

The two communications abilities they decided to concentrate on throughout the year were:

FIGURE 7–3.   *Ali's Letter*

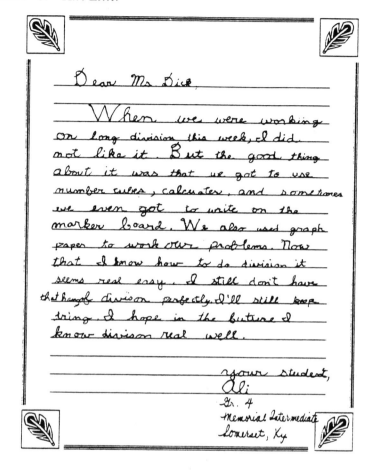

- Students demonstrate an understanding of mathematical concepts by integrating the language of mathematics into their own language.
- Students use physical materials, pictures, symbols, and diagrams to express mathematical ideas.

These two abilities seemed like a good beginning, although they agreed they could now more easily identify another if they felt they needed to.

The communications abilities listed above are *performance standards* as discussed in Chapter 2. As standards for mathematical communication, they represent what these teachers want to build into their lessons and what they want their students to be able to do with respect to communicating in mathematics.

Patty, Sylvia, and Marsha then used a similar process to identify what they wanted their students to work on in patterns and relationships and in mathematical connections. Identifying these performance standards was more difficult, however, because they did not have actual student material to help clarify their thinking and give them a sense of the levels of student performance in these abilities. Instead, they called on their years of classroom experience as well as the NCTM standards documents.

FIGURE 7–4. *Emily's Letter*

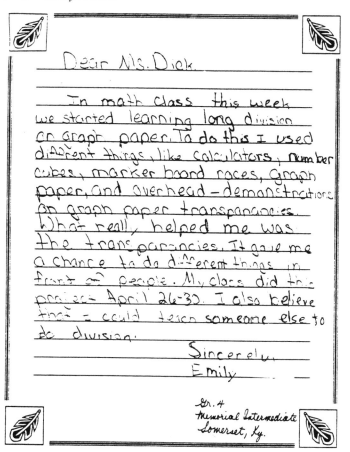

Dear Ms. Dick,

In math class this week we started learning long division on graph paper. To do this I used different things, like calculators, number cubes, marker board races, graph paper, and overhead-demonstrations on graph paper transparancies. What really helped me was the transparancies. It gave me a chance to do different things in front of people. My class did this project April 26-30. I also believe that I could teach someone else to do division.

Sincerely,
Emily

Gr. 4
Memorial Intermediate
Somerset, Ky.

FIGURE 7–5. *Stacy's Letter*

Dear Teacher

This week in math we was intrudusted to Longdivision. first we made up this game with number cubs we also learned the six steps witch are. Divide Multiplie, Subtract, check, Bringdown, then start over. Then we did a few sheets on division Finally on Tuesday we had a checkup to see how we wear doing. finally we had to do a page in the book. Then we had a test and most everyone did well.

By
Stacy

FIGURE 7–6.   *Traci's Letter*

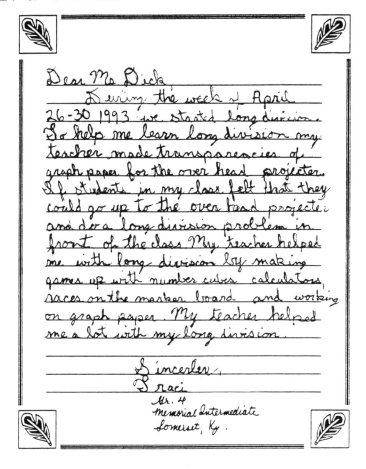

Dear Mr. Dick
During the week of April 26-30 1993 we started long division. To help me learn long division my teacher made transparencies of graph paper for the over head projecter. If students in my class felt that they could go up to the over head projecter and do a long division problem in front of the class My teacher helped me with long division by making games up with number cubes calculators, races on the marker board and working on graph paper. My teacher helped me a lot with my long division.

Sincerely,
Traci
Mr. 4
Memorial Intermediate
Somerset, Ky.

They felt a good beginning performance standard for mathematical connections was the ability to recognize mathematics in other subject areas. They also knew that making this a performance standard meant they had to model these connections in their own teaching in a way they hadn't done before.

In working through the patterns and relationships standards, they reflected on earlier lessons focusing on patterning. Each agreed that students' abilities to recognize patterns and extend patterns were important. Patty pointed out that patterns were found in many subjects—science and language arts (in the sense of repeated themes in stories), for example. She suggested they think of patterns as one of the mathematical connections students would see in other subjects. Marsha and Sylvia agreed they should model these connections in their lessons. They eventually identified two performance standards for patterns and relationships:

• Students demonstrate an ability to represent and describe mathematical

FIGURE 7–7. *Sean's Letter*

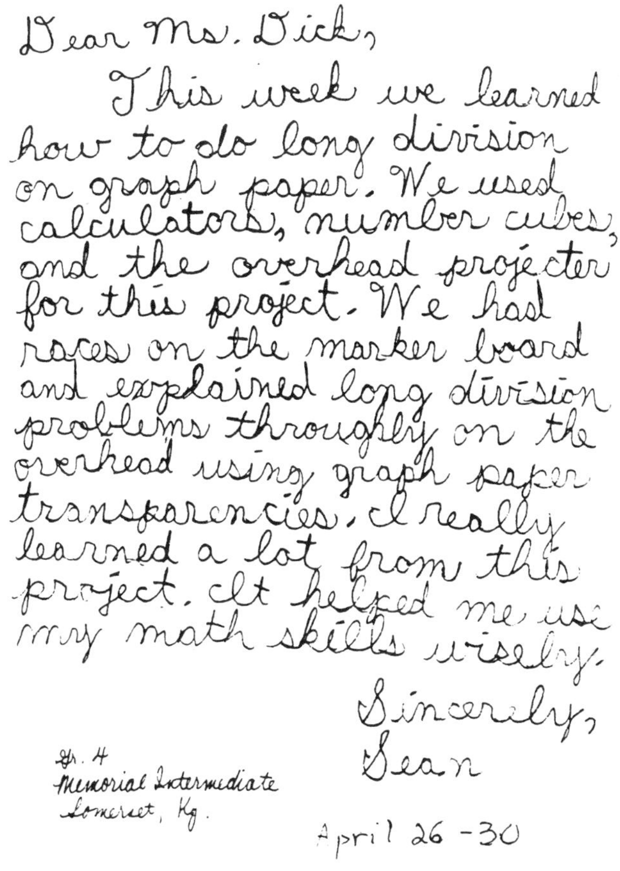

Dear Ms. Dick,

This week we learned how to do long division on graph paper. We used calculators, number cubes, and the overhead projecter for this project. We had races on the marker board and explained long division problems throughly on the overhead using graph paper transparencies. I really learned a lot from this project. It helped me use my math skills wisely.

Sincerily,
Sean

Gr. 4
Memorial Intermediate
Somerset, Ky.

April 26 –30

relationships and use that information to make additional mathematical discoveries.

- Students demonstrate an ability to recognize patterns in a variety of mathematical topics.

Figure 7–8 summarizes the performance standards the teachers agreed would guide their portfolio process and, consequently, their mathematics instruction.

The next step for Marsha, Sylvia, and Patty will be to identify performance indicators for these performance standards. There are two ways they can do this. One, they themselves can decide an appropriate performance continuum for each standard and then share that continuum with the students. Two, they can involve the children in the identification process. An advantage of the second method is that it helps students take ownership not only of the portfolio process but also of its evaluation. To use the second method successfully, you need to

FIGURE 7–8.   *Performance Standards for Third-Grade Portfolios*

Patterns and Relationships in Mathematics
- Demonstrates the ability to represent and describe a mathematical relationship and to use that information to inform further mathematics discoveries.
- Demonstrates the ability to recognize patterns in a variety of mathematical topics.

Mathematical Communications
- Demonstrates an understanding of mathematical concepts by integrating mathematics into their own language.
- Uses physical materials, pictures, symbols, and diagrams to express mathematical ideas.

Mathematical Connections
- Demonstrates the ability to recognize mathematics in other subject areas.
- Demonstrates the ability to recognize connections among topics in mathematics.

remember not to deal with the performance indicators until the students have had an opportunity to understand the performance standards through lessons in which they experience and practice the standards. In other words, it may be difficult for students to understand how they could ever find mathematics in another subject unless they have the experience of doing just that. Many ideas connected with assessment are quite abstract and need to be made as concrete as possible for everyone, especially students. By giving students a role in setting the performance indicators for their portfolio work, you will demystify the assessment process and set down concrete expectations.

What things should I think about in managing the portfolio process?

To manage the portfolio process well, you need to consider a number of important questions:

- What do I want my students to include in their portfolios?
- How can I make portfolios a visible and accessible part of my classroom?
- Where will I find the time to read the portfolios?

You don't have to change your mathematics curriculum totally to accommodate portfolios. Portfolios are designed to capture what you are currently doing in your classroom; then, based on feedback from the portfolios and from other assessment strategies, you may decide to make some adjustments.

Deciding why you want your students to compile portfolios and defining what mathematics you want to emphasize in that process are critical steps, but there are other issues as well. You need to determine how work for the portfolio will be chosen, how it will be organized and presented, and how it will be made accessible to students.

Patty, Sylvia, and Marsha's experiences include some ideas about the selection process. They determined ahead of time the categories of pieces to be included and how the portfolio would be organized, beginning with a table of contents. Many other kinds of pieces or entries can be included in a portfolio. Figure 7–9 lists ideas appropriate for kindergarten through sixth grade. This is not an exhaustive list by any means. We have talked with some teachers who want to include a videotape of a group project as part of the portfolio. Other teachers are talking about how to include material produced by way of computers, calculators, or manipulatives. A portfolio entry is suitable as long as it includes evidence of revision, reflection, and learning over time. An entry with each of these components serves as a springboard for discussing mathematics, learning, strengths and weaknesses, and how to participate in mathematics in a way that tears down walls of isolation for the teacher, the student, and parents.

What do portfolios look like? Most professional people who depend on a portfolio have a leather binder of some kind. In classrooms, what you choose to hold student material will depend on your school budget. Teachers use anything from manila folders to three-ring binders. Some teachers have their students create their own using construction paper or poster board. Hill and Ruptic (1994) suggest stapling two pocketed folders together, one inside the other.

Another management issue is accessibility of the portfolios to your students and to you. Portfolios need to be a visible part of your classroom, and students need to be able to work with them independently. By providing both visibility and accessibility, you make a clear statement that portfolios are an important part of the culture of your classroom.

At the beginning you may need to post portfolio guidelines nearby. Perhaps you and your students will have identified some performance indicators that will help guide their reflections. You may also have specific instructions about how entries should be labeled. Because so much portfolio work is revision, clearly marked dates are very important. Labels may also include assignment titles and descriptions clarifying what the work is about. Labeling requirements

FIGURE 7–9.   *Types of Student Portfolio Pieces*

Writing: journal entries, mathematics autobiographies, letters to the teacher, reflective pieces.

Nonroutine Problems: a problem made up by the student that demonstrates an understanding of the mathematics needed to solve the problem and an ability to provide a reasonable solution strategy.

Revisions: drafts, revisions, and final versions of student work on a complex mathematical problem, including writing, diagrams, graphs, charts, and whatever else is appropriate.

Projects: activities that extend over a period of days or weeks and require a formal presentation of the material in a group or individual format.

Peer Assessment: reflections from classmates on a student's work in relation to performance standards and performance indicators that have been established.

will vary by grade level—clearly more is expected of older than younger students. Whatever you decide is appropriate labeling for your particular grade level may become part of the public notes you keep near your portfolio area.

Managing the portfolio process requires some form of assessment record. Using a standardized form to give students and yourself feedback on portfolio entries will be helpful. Some teachers attach a checklist to the inside of the portfolio folder and use it to keep track of student progress.

Finding the time to read student selections and provide appropriate feedback is very definitely a management issue. It will help if you:

- Ensure that the number of portfolio entries is reasonable.
- Work with your students so that they understand the identified performance standards and performance indicators.
- Make students responsible for providing evidence of meeting performance indicators.

When you first introduce portfolios, three or four selections is a very acceptable goal. The important thing is that each of the entries provides an opportunity for your students to demonstrate evidence of growth in relation to a set of performance standards. You may want your students to develop those three or four entries throughout the entire school year. As you become more confident in the process, however, you'll probably want to increase the number of selections.

When students participate in the assessment process, whether through peer assessment, self-assessment, or both, their collaboration and support makes your work easier. Student involvement only works, however, when they understand what assessment entails and what the performance standards and indicators mean. So you will need to spend time helping your students construct that understanding. It is possible to involve other adults as well. Colleagues, parents, retired teachers, and preservice students at a local college or university are all potential portfolio assessors. You will need to spend some time training them, but once you have done so you will have an ongoing source of support. One of the authors had a very successful experience organizing a pool of retired teachers to assess students. They were flattered to be asked!

How can I use a process folio with a portfolio?

In order for students to have a collection of work from which they can make a selection, they need a place to store it. Many teachers use another kind of folder called a work folder or a process folio. Whatever it's called, the idea is to give students a place to store work they may later decide to include in their portfolio. The contents of these folders will be dictated by the categories for which they will need to make selections. Throughout the semester Sylvia, Patty, and Marsha's students, for example, will collect work related to a group product, an individual product focused on a selected mathematical concept, and a revision. Not every mathematics assignment is included.

Periodically, your students will need to go through the contents of these folders and prioritize their work on the basis of feedback provided either by you as their teacher or by outside assessors. This is an opportunity for you to talk with them about their work and practice reflective questioning.

The following example is from Hill and Ruptic (1994). A class of fifth graders keeps all completed work from the week that pertains to the portfolio categories in a "Friday Folder." Every other Friday, the students take these folders into the hallway and spread out the contents in the order of importance the pieces have for them as learners. Some of this work is revision. The students then write a letter to their parents about their work, answering some of the reflective questions used in class. (The students share these letters with their parents—it is not just an exercise.) In this way, the students gradually choose their final selections for the portfolios.

Whatever method you choose will be a good beginning; just remember that you need some procedure for presorting student work so that the students will be able to make their choices from a reasonable number of pieces.

How can I include students in the portfolio process?

If portfolios are going to be a tool for learning mathematics, students need to have a voice in the process and take an active role. You can give your students that voice and role in several ways.

In assembling a portfolio, students make choices about their work and reflect on this work and these decisions. They select pieces of work for their portfolios relative to categories that you have determined ahead of time or identified after discussions in which the students have taken part. Therefore, an important part of any portfolio process is guiding students in making their choices.

Students need this assistance particularly when they are first learning what revision and reflection mean. (Student reflection is dealt with more thoroughly in Chapter 8.) They need practice and feedback in critiquing their own work and the work of others with more than a superficial "I chose this piece because I did a good job." When students select work they believe is their best piece of mathematical communication, you may need to probe a bit into why they believe this to be so. Individual conferences or whole-class discussions about the performance indicators related to mathematical communications will help them understand what contributes to a best piece.

Lambdin and Walker (1994) include an excellent discussion about the guidance students need in being reflective and the obstacles facing a portfolio program until they receive that guidance. They suggest identifying questions that will help students think reflectively about their portfolio selections. These questions should be related to the performance standards you are emphasizing as well as to the kind of entries the students are selecting. Examples of some general questions that may help students think more reflectively include:

- Why did you select this piece?
- What did you learn in doing this mathematics task that you did not know before?
- What does this piece show about you as a mathematician?
- When you revised this piece of work, what did you do? Why did you do that?
- In which part of this activity/task do you think you need more practice?
- What would make this an easier task for you to do?
- What part of this task did you like best? Why?

These kinds of questions act as prompts to help guide student thinking. (If you are teaching very young children, you can write down your students' oral reflections and include those in the portfolio.) Once students have begun to internalize these prompts, you can stop using them or revise them.

Another strategy is to put an example of student work, perhaps someone your students don't know, on an overhead and talk as a class about why the student selected it as a best piece. During this conversation, you will model how to think about work in a way that moves your students past concerns about right and wrong answers. You'll also point out that good work takes time and is ongoing.

The process of building students' reflective skills does not happen overnight. You need to be patient. Most children are not comfortable trusting their own judgment and they do not have much experience in applying standards to their own work. Today's students are used to relying on others, particularly adults, to tell them which is their best piece of work.

How can I share portfolios with families and the community?

Portfolios usually contain such rich information that you will want to share them with the families of your students and with others in your school community. Portfolios may or may not count toward a letter grade. Whether they do or not is a separate issue from wanting to share the student's learning and to model to families and the community the process of mathematics that goes beyond getting correct numerical answers. Again, there are no right or wrong ways to engage in this sharing. And you may not be ready to share until you have worked with portfolios for a year or two. You are the best judge for when the time is right.

Some teachers hold "portfolio evenings" and invite the families of their students to school. Each family takes the student's portfolio and spreads it out on the floor, listening to and talking with the student. This gives students, family members, and teachers an opportunity to explore the portfolio process. By inviting families to school, you can more easily consolidate your time and don't have to organize individual reports to send home. When you devote an evening to portfolios, you are making a statement that portfolios are an important part of your mathematics instruction. Since most parents will not have had portfolios as students, that message may be important for them to hear.

You could also decide to send portfolios home at intervals throughout the year with a letter to parents outlining what the class has been working on.

Often, teachers send portfolios on to the teachers the students will have next year. This provides excellent continuity for the student and supplements the numerical data found in student records. An alternate idea is to have each student present his or her portfolio to next year's teachers in a special session just for this purpose.

There is no right way to do portfolios. Portfolios are a process for evaluating your students' growth in mathematics, for documenting their strengths and weaknesses, and for informing your instruction. You do not have to redo your entire mathematics curriculum in order to integrate portfolios into your classroom. Learning how to work with portfolios is a combination of trial and error, your own beliefs about what is important in mathematics, and patience with your children as they learn how to become reflective learners. A portfolio is one of many different kinds of assessment strategies, all of which need time to develop. We have suggested ideas about how to get started, how to manage the process once it is underway, and how to involve students and the larger community. Once you've inaugurated the portfolio process, you will be impressed by the kinds of information about your students they can provide. Be patient!

· 8 ·

Making Students Part of the Assessment Process: Encouraging Self-Assessment

How effectively can self-assessment be used in first or second grade?

IN THIS CHAPTER

- Why is self-assessment emerging as an important part of alternative assessment?
- What is self-assessment?
- How is reflection linked to self-assessment?
- What part does reflection play in developing good self-assessment skills?
- How can I encourage reflection in very young children who do not seem developmentally ready?
- What is the role of performance indicators in the self-assessment process?
- How can peer assessment contribute to students' understanding of themselves as learners?

KEY TERMS

Self-assessment in education means taking the time to understand who and where one is as a learner. When students reflect on their learning experience, noting what happened, what they learned, how it was different from other learning experiences, what was confusing, in what parts of the experience they had the greatest success, they are engaged in self-assessment.

In **peer assessment,** classmates have an opportunity to reflect on one another's work according to criteria with which they are familiar and which makes sense to them.

Scaffolding is a term often used to describe building up a student's mental network of ideas over time. This scaffold or network provides a student with a conceptual understanding of more abstract ideas.

Debriefing is a strategy for guiding students through a self-assessment or peer assessment process. Debriefing is structured around a number of open-ended questions designed to help students think about the learning task just completed.

Why is self-assessment emerging as an important part of alternative assessment?

Remember your own days as an elementary student? That's longer ago for some than for others, but you probably recall the anxiety you felt when your teacher returned a recently taken mathematics test. Why were these occasions so fraught with fear?

In part, feelings of anxiousness arise because most children want to do well in school. They are afraid of failure and the embarrassment of not appearing as "smart" as their peers. Being a good student in mathematics is often equated with getting all the answers correct on a test. Further, students do not always have a sense of what they do or do not know in mathematics. When students are not sure of their individual strengths and weaknesses in mathematics, taking a test can be a very mysterious process.

In talking with teachers, we find that for some the association between mystery and mathematics is very strong. At an inservice session for elementary teachers a short while ago, we were discussing children's attitudes toward mathematics. One teacher recalled her childhood belief that mathematics was not to be understood, only suffered through, and admitted to still feeling a little that way as an adult. As a child, she believed that her classmates who did well in math somehow knew certain "tricks" that helped them get the right answers. This teacher is undoubtedly not alone in feeling that mathematics and magic are closely related.

How can such myths and associations be debunked? Linking mathematics assessment and instruction more clearly and consistently erodes old myths about magic, mysteries, and getting good grades. Performance assessment gives students the opportunity to become active participants in the evaluation of their own work, an evaluation that is interpreted as more than right or wrong answers. Self-assessment seems such a simple concept—empowering children with reflective strategies that will help them understand themselves as learners of mathematics. What could make more sense? Yet it is something the education community has neglected for decades.

What is self-assessment?

Self-assessment is reflecting about an experience in which we were a participant, whether that experience took place inside or outside the classroom. When we take the time to reflect in a guided way on that experience, noting what hap-

FIGURE 8–1. *The Process of Student Self-Assessment*

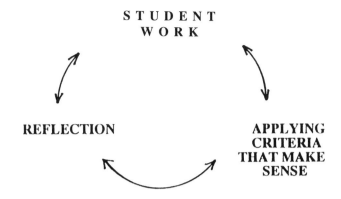

pened, what we learned from it, how it was different from other experiences, we are engaged in self-assessment. Self-assessment allows children to become more conscious of, intentional in, and observant of their own learning.

In order for students to self-assess their work, they need to develop two complementary abilities: the ability to engage in focused reflection and the ability to apply criteria or performance indicators to their work objectively. This is shown schematically in Figure 8–1.

How is reflection linked to self-assessment?

Think about what you do when you are being reflective about one of your own learning experiences. You probably ask yourself a series of mental questions: What did I learn? What do I need to practice more? What did I enjoy? Why was this confusing? When did I do something like this before? In asking yourself these questions, you come up with some insights about yourself as a learner. You get a sense of how you're doing in relationship to what you are trying to learn. The same process should happen with your students when learning mathematics. Figure 8–2 lists some examples of self-assessment questions.

Self-assessment goes beyond describing how students feel about a learning experience. It is intended to help students understand their strengths and weaknesses as learners by being as objective as possible about their performances on

FIGURE 8–2. *Example of Self-Assessment Questions*

- What do I need to know in order to do this task?
- What is familiar about this task?
- How do I feel when I am doing this task?
- What is getting easier?
- How would I describe my strengths?
- What is still hard for me?
- What would help me improve?
- What did I learn?

a given task. Whatever their age, everyone has a set of metacognitive capabilities that allows them to monitor their experiences. However, this monitoring capacity needs to be guided and practiced if it is to develop to its full potential. It is unfair to expect children to have a well-developed capacity for monitoring their learning unless the appropriate practice and feedback is provided. Helping children become aware of their own learning and why that awareness is an important dimension of learning is essential to building the relationship between learning and assessment. When a student has the ability to reflect on his own learning, he can move from concentrating only on the outcome of learning—"How many did I get wrong?"—to addressing the actions that produced the outcome.

Unfortunately, asking children to reflect on how they learn and what they are learning has not been a priority in many school systems. Consider the following vignette:

PARENT: What did you learn at school today?
SEVEN-YEAR-OLD: Nuthin.
PARENT: Hm. Tell me what you did all day.
SEVEN-YEAR-OLD: Well, mm, it's kinda hard to explain.
PARENT: What subjects did you have?
SEVEN-YEAR-OLD: Spelling and math.
PARENT: What did you do?
SEVEN-YEAR-OLD: Well . . . the teacher wrote things on the board and we put them on our paper.

No doubt something really did happen for this child in terms of learning, but she obviously has little experience articulating her thoughts about what learning is for her. She can describe activities but not in a particularly reflective way, a way that gives a sense of her as a learner and the process she moves through as she is learning.

What part does reflection play in developing good self-assessment skills?

Teachers and parents can play a significant role in providing students with opportunities to practice reflective skills. One strategy that you can use in the classroom or suggest to parents is called "Thinking Aloud" (Diez and Moon 1990).

To use this strategy, group your students into pairs, a thinker and a listener, and give them a problem similar to this one: What day follows the day before yesterday if two days from now will be Sunday? The thinker says aloud what goes through her mind while she attempts to solve the problem. The other student listens with full attention, asking questions only to help clarify what the thinker has said. When the pair has an answer, the listener explains to the whole class what the thinker did and why.

Next conduct a debriefing period during which you and your students focus on the process of how everyone arrived at the answers they did. The correct answer (Thursday, in the example) is a minimal part of the debriefing. You want to concentrate on asking questions that will invite students to share the ways in which they went about solving the riddle: What was the first strategy you tried? What worked and what did not work with that strategy? What did you try next? Why?

You may find that some students have drawn a diagram to help them visualize the information given in the problem. You may discover that others have missed critical information in the question: they may have failed to recognize that the problem asks for the day that *follows* the day before yesterday and concentrated instead on the day before yesterday.

Thinking aloud in this kind of exercise helps students recognize that different strategies can be used to generate a solution as well as to make their own thinking processes concrete. Students will also come to understand the importance of thinking about the process used to solve a problem, not just the answer to the problem. By focusing on the process, you tell your students that reflecting on that process is valuable and at the same time give them the opportunity to practice self-assessing their learning.

"Connection Making" (Diez and Moon 1990) is another strategy that gives students ongoing practice in reflection and, consequently, in self-assessment. In connection making, students create links between and among elements in the learning process and themselves as learners. For example, it is important for students to understand the connection between the mathematics learned in school and how that mathematics is applied in everyday life. Lauren Resnick (1987) gives a wonderful example of connection making in which children practice making mathematical judgments in everyday contexts. In her illustration, fourth graders are given a quarter, a dime, and two pennies and asked how much more money they need to buy an ice cream cone that costs sixty cents. Most quickly answer a quarter. From a real-world perspective, adding a quarter is the simplest way to round the total to sixty cents. The exact answer, however, is twenty-three cents. Real-life applications help children understand how numbers are used in everyday situations and emphasize that the best solutions are not always exact ones.

Connection-making exercises give students a chance to build self-confidence in their ability to provide a rationale for mathematical solutions, a critical component of self-assessment. When students articulate the choices they make, they are "assessing" their understanding of life and the things they have learned that guide their choices.

How can I encourage reflection in very young children who do not seem developmentally ready?

Children in kindergarten or first grade certainly cannot develop the reflective behaviors children in fourth or fifth grade exhibit, but they do have potential. Children at any age are building cognitive networks based on experiences and information that make sense to them. Making sense involves being reflective, even at younger ages. If you are a teacher of very young children, you will have to spend more time modeling self-assessment behaviors. This is time well spent, however, since it helps students construct an important foundation on which they can build their self-assessment sophistication as they mature.

Kindergarten through second-grade teachers can ensure that their students experience self-assessment by asking them questions: What did you learn? What was hard for you? Why do you think that was hard? What was easy for you? When did we do something like this before? How is this different from what we did before? Pose these questions in whatever format works best in your class—whole-group, small-group, or one-to-one. The primary purpose is to give children an opportunity to hear these thoughtful questions and to see them as a natural extension of any learning experience. These scaffolding questions make it possible for students to ask similar questions of themselves as their reflective capacities mature across grade levels.

When children are learning how to respond to questions like these, you may want to provide prompts to stimulate and clarify their thinking even further. For example, when you ask a student what was hard about a particular mathematical task, perhaps developing a pattern of her own, she may respond, "Everything!" This gives you a clear idea how she feels about the task, but it doesn't tell you what about it was difficult. Try to get underneath that kind of global response and discover what *everything* means. You might ask, What were you doing when you felt things getting hard? or Can you show me how you started your task? or Have you done anything like this before? Young children, lacking well-developed analytic skills and living their life much in the present moment, often mix up how they feel about a task with understanding the skills required to do a task. This distinction is really a lifelong learning process! But we can help students a great deal by modeling this distinction for them at an early age.

Making this distinction is not saying that the way children feel about mathematical tasks is unimportant; recognizing those feelings is valid, and you should spend time exploring those feelings in your class. Math anxiety is a very real problem. At the same time, it is critical for children to learn how to sort out how they feel about a task from the skills and abilities they need to do that task successfully. The reflective component of self-assessment is an excellent strategy by which children can learn to recognize and appreciate the distinction.

Figure 8–3 is a self-assessment idea that can be used with younger students toward the end of the school year. If writing is an issue, responses can be

FIGURE 8–3.   *Math Self-Assessment Activity*

The teacher you will have for next year is very interested in getting to know you better. If you answer these questions it will help this teacher understand your experiences in math this year.

What do you think are the things you do best in math?

I learned (describe at least two things) in math this year:

What are the things you need help with in math?

How do you feel when you are doing math activities?

What do you want to work on next year in math?

Note: If your students are too young to respond to these questions, have them draw a picture of themselves doing math. Arrange their pictures in a display and spend time asking some of the questions listed above, making notes for your records as well as for next year's teachers.

obtained in an interview. Perhaps a parent or grandparent would be willing to come to your class for a week and help you with the interviews. Some work produced by third graders in response to a similar self-assessment task is shown in Figures 8–4 through 8–9.

What is the role of performance indicators in the self-assessment process?

As reflection becomes a more natural part of the learning process, students will better understand how to use performance indicators or criteria in judging their own performance. Performance indicators serve as a mirror, reflecting an individual student in action as a way to help other students, teachers, and parents judge how that student is doing in relation to an identified ability. That reflection is formed when what the student does—the actions she takes in her mathematics classes—is held up against performance indicators that make up a continuum of benchmarks for an identified ability. It is this descriptive picture of performance, their own and their classmates', that gives students objective data about themselves as learners, taking the mystery out of the learning process and making it concrete.

Let's take what we have just said about using performance indicators as a mirror and put it in the context of your classroom. For example, if you identify making mathematical connections as an important performance standard, then you will need to make sure that your students understand what you mean by mathematical connections and the performance indicators you will use as benchmarks to assess their developing abilities to make mathematical connections. Suppose you explain to your students that when someone makes mathematical connections, she is able to understand how mathematics is used in everyday life. Brainstorm with them about how they use mathematics when they are not in school. Talk about ways in which the mathematics done in school can sometimes be different from the mathematics used in real life and why that is the case. Write down the important ideas generated during these discussions and display them where your students can refer to them whenever they like. As

FIGURE 8–4. *Casey's Self-Assessment*

Next year you will have a new teacher. Introduce yourself as a math student to your new teacher. Try to answer the following questions in your introduction.

I like to do *Fact Familysthe* best

I need more help with *Writing wordproblems*

I am best at *Borrowing*

I get confused when *write about myself*

This school year I think I have grown the most in *multiplcataion*

FIGURE 8–5. *Mike's Self-Assessment*

Next year you will have a new teacher. Introduce yourself as a math student to your new teacher. Try to answer the following questions in your introduction.

I like to do ____*division*____ best

I need more help with *fractions* _____

I am best at ____*division*____

I get confused when *one person has one answer one person has another*

This school year I think I have grown the most in *times tables*

you introduce mathematics lessons that contain examples of applying mathematics skills in everyday life, they will experience these ideas in very concrete ways. Soon your students will develop a grasp of what is meant by connecting mathematics to everyday living.

Once your students can talk about ideas central to making connections, they can begin to participate with you in identifying performance indicators for making mathematical connections in everyday contexts. A third-grade class focusing on the connections standard decided on the following set of performance indicators:

Acceptable evidence of making mathematical connections:

Being able to talk or write about how I use measurement, numbers, data, and estimation when I am not in school in a way that makes sense to my teacher, my classmates, and myself.

Not acceptable evidence of making mathematical connections:

Not being able to talk or write about how I use measurement, numbers, data, and estimation when I am not in school in a way that make sense to my teacher, my classmates, and myself; having to be reminded all the time to look for mathematical connections outside of school.

A fourth-grade teacher shared this story about making mathematical connections: Her class was working in small groups on a problem involving buying fish for an aquarium. The students were given a fixed amount of money to spend for the aquarium and a list of how much certain types of fish cost. Three students negotiating a spending decision were discussing the cost of three fish at twenty-seven cents each. Thomas and Jeff used the traditional multiplication algorithm, 3×27. Stacey figured it out buy adding 27 plus 27 and getting 54, then adding another 27 for a total of 81 cents. She told the boys she could not do it their way and explained how she did it her way. The boys, at first skeptical, finally accepted Stacey's reasoning because she came up with the same

FIGURE 8–6.   *Frankie's Self-Assessment*

Next year you will have a new teacher. Introduce yourself as a math student to your new teacher. Try to answer the following questions in your introduction.

I like to do _labs in groups_ best

I need more help with _multipacation Facts_

I am best at _divison_

I get confused when _we talk about how many combonations.._

This school year I think I have grown the most in _working with other kids._

FIGURE 8–7.   *Amanda's Self-Assessment*

Next year you will have a new teacher. Introduce yourself as a math student to your new teacher. Try to answer the following questions in your introduction.

I like to do _geometry_ best

I need more help with _deviding with remaiders_

I am best at _broiwing_

I get confused when _people start adding all these larg numbe to anser questions_

This school year I think I have grown the most in _sitting to a problm and not giving up._

answer they did. Stacey was able to talk about making connections between addition and her mathematical task in a way that gave her classmates acceptable evidence that she understood the mathematics.

The process of learning mathematics and being assessed on what they have learned will be less mysterious to children when the following features are part of every classroom:

- Children are familiar with the standards of performance in mathematics their teachers want them to demonstrate.
- Children have some role in helping set the performance indicators for some of those standards.

FIGURE 8–8.   *Leah's Self-Assessment*

Next year you will have a new teacher. Introduce yourself as a math student to your new teacher. Try to answer the following questions in your introduction.

I like to do _3D shapes_ best

I need more help with _some word problems_

I am best at _building a table_

I get confused when _I don't pay attention right away_

This school year I think I have grown the most in _Multipcation_

FIGURE 8–9.   *Brian's Self-Assessment*

Next year you will have a new teacher. Introduce yourself as a math student to your new teacher. Try to answer the following questions in your introduction.

I like to do _multion_ best

I need more help with _disvin_

I am best at _working with grups_

I get confused when _we do dizvin_

This school year I think I have grown the most in _maltial ration_

- Children have consistent opportunities to practice identified standards of performance in mathematics.
- Children receive consistent feedback from their teacher, their peers, and themselves during mathematical practice and at the conclusion of formal assessments.

In a classroom where assessment has a central place in the instructional process, the focus shifts from giving tests to helping students understand the goals of a learning experience and the criteria for successfully completing that experience. Self-assessment is central to this process. Through self-assessment, students take part in the instruction process by evaluating their own performances.

How can peer assessment contribute to students' understanding of themselves as learners?

Building a reflective community in your classroom also involves providing opportunities for students to think about and respond to the work of their classmates. Peer assessment is an extension of self-assessment in that it gives "the self," the student, occasions to share his understanding of a mathematics task with other students. In the process of sharing, students spend time thinking about their understanding in an effort to evaluate the performance of another student. It is a wonderfully rich process.

Peer assessment is easily folded into self-assessment when the same criteria are used for both. If your class has agreed to some general criteria about communications in mathematics, then those criteria should be used for all assessments—self, peer, informal, and formal.

Figures 8–10 through 8–16 are examples of peer assessments made by second through fourth graders. Students were asked to respond to another student's work by showing or telling ways in which the other student might better understand addition. The richness of such a task is the evidence it provides about your students' understanding of addition. It also gives you a sample of how well they are able to communicate that understanding. Finally, it gives your students a wonderful opportunity to assess another student's work in an objective manner. As you read through these peer assessments, notice how the students go beyond telling Mike or Ben he was wrong to trying to structure an explanation that might be of some real assistance. While there are differences in the style and sophistication of these explanations, it is important to remember

FIGURE 8–10.   *Misha's Peer Assessment*

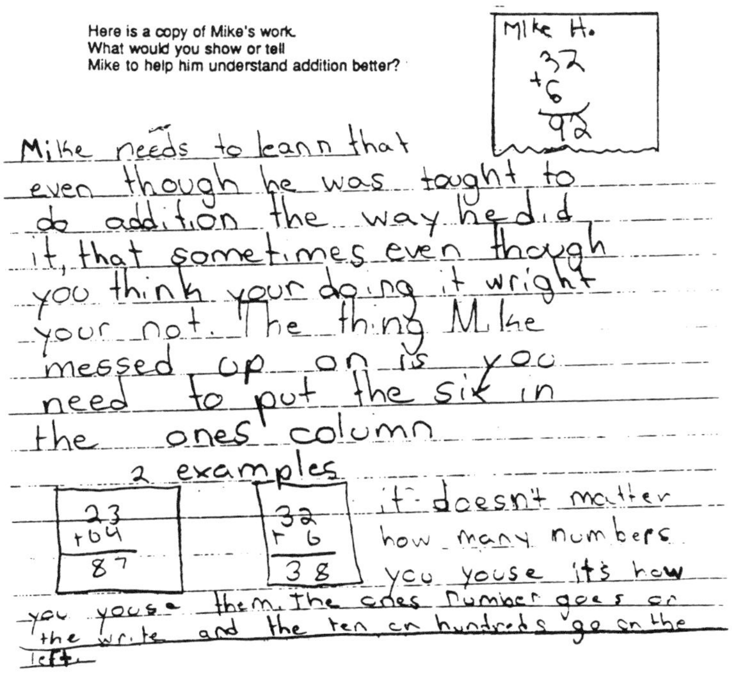

that the students were using their mathematical experience to help Mike and Ben.

Having students help other students by sharing their mathematical knowledge and experience is perhaps the most critical process in peer assessment and the thing that distinguishes it from any other assessment activity. Peer assessment grows out of serious student reflection, so the opportunity to create reflective strategies in your classroom is an essential part of the entire alternative assessment concept.

If assessment means "sitting down beside" (see Chapter 2), then self-assessment means sitting with yourself and taking the time to understand who you are as a learner. This understanding can only come through practice: students need to be given time, opportunity, and models for being reflective about their learning. Don't be discouraged if your students' responses are not as rich as you think they could be. Students often are not used to being asked reflective questions. Traditionally students have not been asked to play a role in their own evaluation. The process of self-assessment changes this tradition. When self-assessment becomes part of your mathematics program, your students will grow in three important areas: in becoming an independent learner, in gaining insight into their own learning, and in showing more initiative and interest in the learning process.

FIGURE 8–11.   *Heather's Peer Assessment*

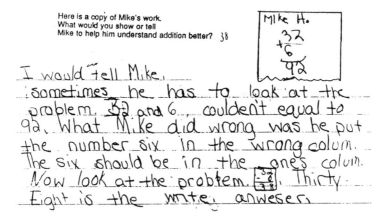

FIGURE 8–12.   *Kent's Peer Assessment*

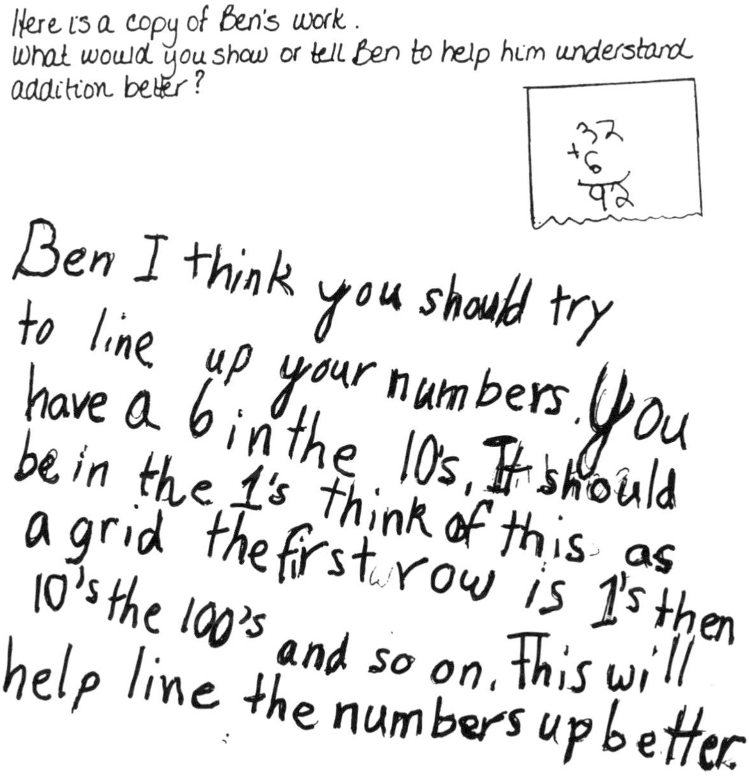

Here is a copy of Ben's work.
What would you show or tell Ben to help him understand
addition better?

```
 37
+ 6
 92
```

Ben I think you should try
to line up your numbers. You
have a 6 in the 10's. It should
be in the 1's think of this as
a grid the first row is 1's then
10's the 100's and so on. This will
help line the numbers up better.

FIGURE 8–13. *Tim's Peer Assessment*

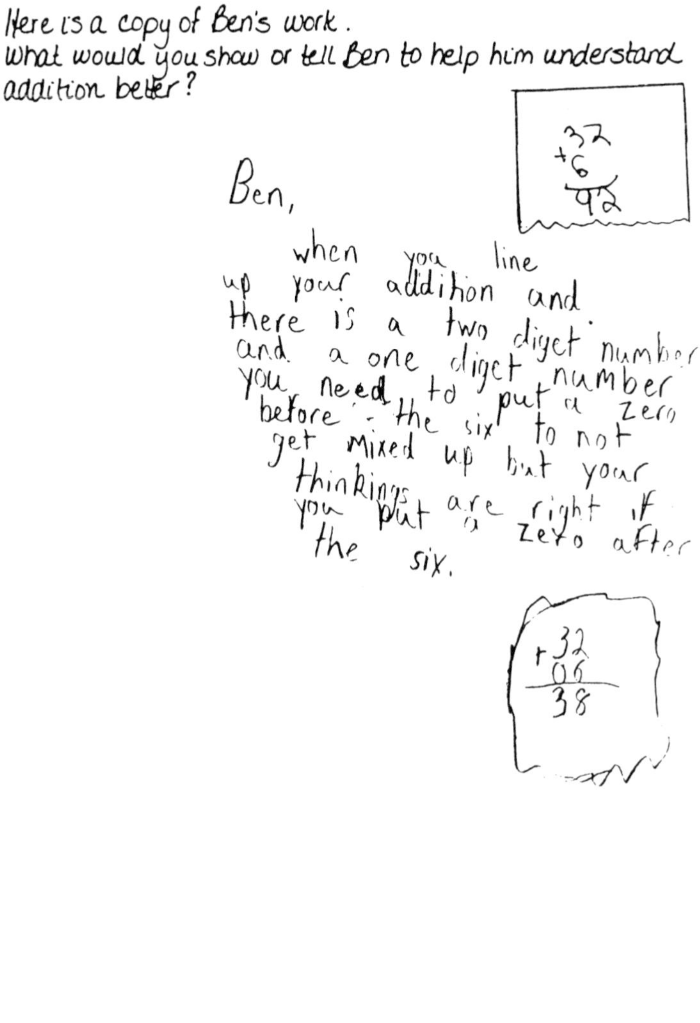
Here is a copy of Ben's work.
What would you show or tell Ben to help him understand addition better?

32
+6
92

Ben,

when you line up your addition and there is a two diget number and a one diget number you need to put a zero before the six to not get mixed up but your thinkings are right if you put a zero after the six.

+32
06
38

FIGURE 8–14. *Peter's Peer Assessment*

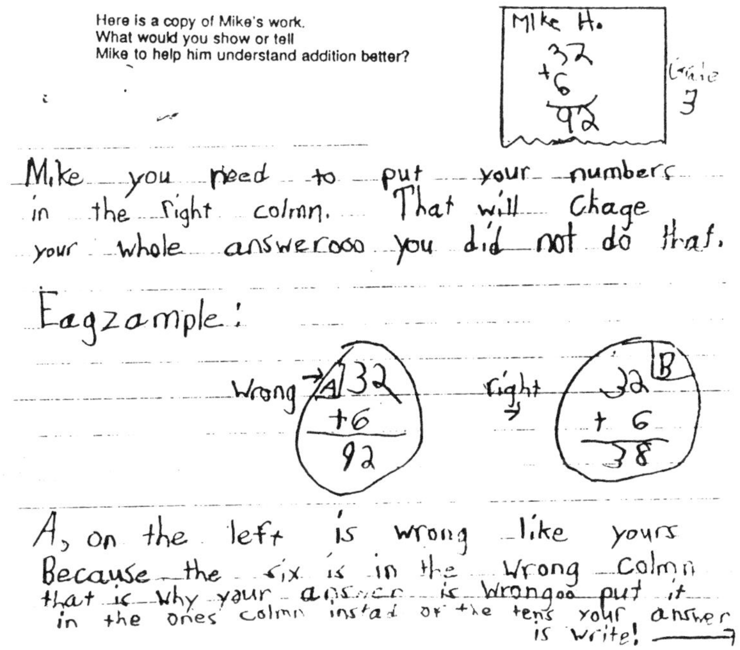

Here is a copy of Mike's work.
What would you show or tell
Mike to help him understand addition better?

Mike H.
  32
 + 6
  92

Mike you need to put your numbers in the right colmn. That will chage your whole answerooo you did not do that.

Eagzample:

Wrong →A 32
        + 6
         92

right → 32 B
       + 6
        38

A, on the left is wrong like yours Because the six is in the wrong colmn that is why your answer is wrongoo put it in the ones colmn instad ot the tens your answer is write! ———→

FIGURE 8–15.   *Elizabeth's Peer Assessment*

Here is a copy of Ben's work.
What would you show or tell Ben to help him understand
addition better?

In addition, you put the
smallest number, over to the
right side. Then, if you do that, this is
what the problem should look like =

'32
+ 6 . Now, he can do the problem,

And the answer is 38. Addition is
really very simple, if you line up
your numbers carefully, and
answer them correctly, and
you will do it perfectly!!

FIGURE 8–16. *Heather's Peer Assessment*

Here is a copy of Mike's work.
What would you show or tell
Mike to help him understand addition better?

Mike H.
32
+6
92

Dear Mike,
          The first thing you have to do with
your problem is to put the six in the
ones colum. That would change it arowr.
Then you would have to change
your answer To point out ta you, if
you count up on your fingers 6 more to
32 you would end up with 38.
When you have a onedidgit number, and
your adding it to a 2didgit number the one
didgit will always be in the ones
place. $\frac{32}{+6}$ $\frac{}{38}$ You can also use counters.
                        To use counters you can use
beans, pennies, or any thing little, Now you need to

to lay out 32 counters to find the answer you will add
6. To make sure you have 32 counters to begin with
you can make 3 groups of ten add 2 and you've
got 32. Now add six,

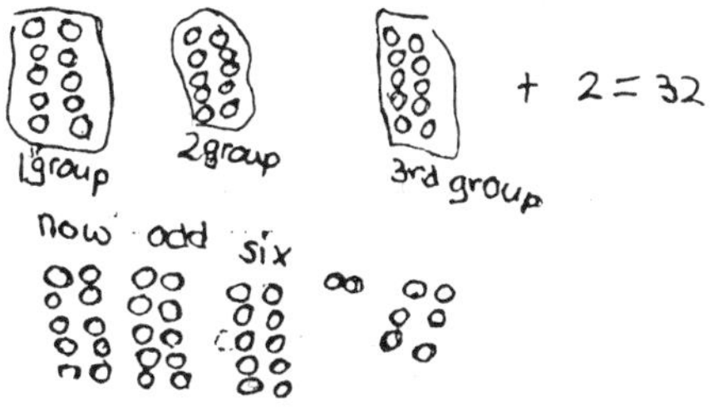

1 group   2 group   3rd group   + 2 = 32

now add six

· 9 ·

Reporting Assessment Information

This is the second year I've used portfolios in my classroom. Last year, I didn't include the portfolios in my grading process. I thought of them as one part of my classroom and report cards as another, separate component. But this year I want to include portfolios in my grading process. I'm just not sure how to do it.

IN THIS CHAPTER

- How can I involve parents in the learning and assessment processes of my classroom?
- What do I do about report cards?
- How do assessment strategies affect accountability?
- How do assessment strategies figure in program evaluations?
- How do new reporting systems relate to my teaching?

KEY TERMS

To **aggregate** means to put data together or gather it into a whole in an effort to find patterns or trends. Generally, data from the same assessment tasks are grouped together to depict performance patterns across students, either numerically or descriptively.

Evaluation is the process of making judgments based on the evidence gathered from assessment strategies.

Value-added assessment involves identifying a current level of performance and then reexamining the performance level after a particular experience to determine the value added by that experience.

Normal distribution curve refers to the distribution of a population with respect to a particular variable. A normal distribution is symmetrical and the mean, mode, and median all lie at the peak of the curve. It is sometimes referred to as a bell-shaped curve.

Thus far, we have focused on how you can use assessment data in your classroom. Assessment data also inform other interested parties of your students' knowledge and understanding of mathematics. This chapter focuses on the ways in which different types of assessment data are reported to diverse audiences. Parents want to know how their children are doing, and schools, districts, states, and the nation require assessment data for accountability purposes. Whenever possible, you want to develop ways to report student growth that do not compromise the intent of new assessment strategies but do meet a variety of reporting requirements.

How can I involve parents in the learning and assessment processes in my classroom?

As teachers, you most frequently report students' learning progress to their parents. (Since many children live in homes where the primary caregiver is not the parent, *parent* here refers to role rather than the biological relationship.) You also probably have more control over how assessment information is shared with parents than how it is reported for accountability purposes.

Keeping parents informed about the instruction and assessment practices of your classroom helps strengthen the home-school connection. Providing regular opportunities for families to communicate with you encourages them to become involved in your classroom and acknowledge the responsibility they share for educating their children. This communication may also help you better meet the needs of individual students. It lets families know that you value their input and lets them in on the rationale behind your classroom practices so that they can support your efforts. It may prompt family members to become advocates for your policies and approaches, reinforce your instructional and assessment strategies at home, and offer to come into your classroom to help you administer new instructional and assessment practices.

Before their children enter school, parents are very conscious of assessing and documenting learning and growth. First smiles, steps, and words, likes and dislikes, are observed and are often recorded in a "baby book." True, when young children are cared for outside the home, sometimes the caregiver sees the baby do something for the first time. However, the baby quickly repeats the feat at home, allowing the parents to see the evidence and validate the ability themselves.

Day-care activities are usually similar to those at home. Many activities in school may not be, however, particularly as the student progresses through the grades. Parents may not have the opportunity to validate their children's ability to form number sentences, make a graph, or use a spreadsheet. In day-care, furthermore, parents usually pick up and drop off their children every day, moments that allow them to exchange comments and information with the caregiver. In elementary school, parents become more removed from the daily goings-on in the classroom and from the assessment of their children and are thus more dependent on school-based reporting mechanisms.

Even though they depend on your reports, parents often have firm convictions about the form these reports should take and the aspects of classroom learning they should emphasize. Their own schooling experiences have led them to expect how things are going to be done. They may have particular expectations about what it means to be a successful learner of mathematics and how mathematics is taught. If you challenge these preconceived notions, you create anxiety because parents want to make sure their children get the skills they assume are needed for later success. In fact, "the more you depart from traditional curriculum, testing, and report cards, the greater the need to communicate with parents" (Hill and Ruptic 1994, p. 204).

For an example, we can look back to the 1960s when "new math" was introduced in the schools. One of its major problems was parental reaction. Many parents could no longer help their second-grade children with their mathematics homework, and they responded in various ways. Some said it made them feel stupid and they stopped offering to help. Some became angry. They couldn't imagine why the school was teaching their children this material. It couldn't be valuable—they hadn't needed it. A few schools actively involved the parents in the mathematics reform, helping them understand the goals of the program and why it was needed. School personnel taught parents the mathematics involved, relating it to mathematics they already knew. These parents were able to support the schools and their children. Unfortunately, this didn't happen very often.

The current reform effort in mathematics is occurring in ways very different from the reform movement of the sixties. Of particular note is that unlike the sixties, teachers have been intricately involved in developing and implementing the new standards.

Parents must also be involved. The first task is to tell parents what they can expect from your mathematics classroom. Teachers often use a letter of introduction to begin communicating about this issue. An example is provided in Figure 9–1. The letter offers a general view of the mathematics classroom in terms most parents can understand and yet does not talk down to them. It also provides specific suggestions for parent-led activities that will support their children's learning.

Many teachers continue to write informative newsletters throughout the year. A kindergarten teacher created the examples in Figures 9–2 and 9–3. Notes and telephone calls can also continue the rapport you have established with the parents, letting them know you want them to be aware of what's going on in your classroom.

You can show parents that you value their knowledge and involvement by asking them to complete a questionnaire about their children (this questionnaire can be sent home with your introductory letter). An example of a questionnaire—purposely kept to a single page—is provided in Figure 9–4. You can learn a lot about a child's disposition toward mathematics by learning about a child's activities at home. Doing puzzles, building with blocks, and sorting collections are home activities that may suggest an interest in mathematics.

Parents also learn about your mathematics classroom from the homework you assign. Homework assignments that include open-ended questions, investigations, reflective writing, and self-assessment inform parents that you find these activities essential to learning mathematics. You can also involve parents in the assessment process more directly by sending home an interview for students to

FIGURE 9–1.   *Sample Letter to Parents*

Dear Parents,

This is always an exciting time of year for me. I look forward to greeting an enthusiastic group of children next week, who are eager to learn and make new friends. As the result of a workshop I attended this summer, I am also particularly excited about exploring mathematics with your children. I would like to share with you a few things about the way mathematics will be taught this year.

My primary goal for mathematics is to have students develop powerful ways to do mathematics and to be able to communicate their mathematical thinking. Your children will be involved in mathematical investigations that allow them to develop their mathematical ideas. The investigations will be active. Your children will be counting, sorting, ordering, measuring, and manipulating shapes as well as talking, drawing, and writing about their ideas.

Since there will be a greater focus on exploration, your child may not bring home a math paper every day. This certainly doesn't mean that no mathematics was done! For example, on the first day of school your child will be doing an estimation activity with beans. The children will try to take a handful of ten beans from a jar. Each handful will be counted and graphed as to whether the number was less than ten, exactly ten, or greater than ten. We will talk about the activity and discuss our graphs. Significant mathematics learning will take place, but there will not be a worksheet to take home.

Estimating is an important mathematical skill that you can help support at home. Everyday questions (How many raisins do you think are in this box? How long do you think this box of cereal will last? How many walking steps will it take us to reach the mailbox?) help to develop your child's sense of number. As the year progresses we will also be exploring shapes, time, measurement, and money. I will keep you informed by sending you periodic newsletters.

As you may know, there is an open house planned for later in September, so that you can learn more about the expectations and curriculum of your child's classroom. Later in the fall, parent-teacher conferences are held. In the meantime, please feel free to call or visit the classroom. I look forward to our working together to ensure that your child has a successful year in the second grade.

Sincerely,

---

complete with their parents. The interview guide in Figure 9–5, for example, supports an assignment asking children to keep a record of the specific times and total amount of time family members spend reading during one week, to display the data in a graph, and to write about what they learned from this data.

You may also be able to involve parents in the assessment process by virtue of their professions. Successfully communicating mathematical ideas is related to the audience to whom those ideas are expressed. Imagine classroom investigations that require students to collect data about traffic at various intersections and make a recommendation to the town traffic officer about whether or not traffic lights are needed, to collect data about reading preferences compared with the books in the school or town library and write to the librarian about

FIGURE 9–2.   *Becky's October 8 Newsletter*

ROOM 110 NEWS   October 8, 1992

Dear Parents:

Looking back over the last two weeks, much has happened in our classroom. First, let me say thank you for joining us at Open House. It was wonderful to see so many of you, to hear your kind words and thoughtful questions. Your support and concerns help to make our school an exceptional place where children can feel safe and ready to learn.

I know many of you had a chance to read our, <u>Kindergarten, Kindergarten, Who Do You See?</u> book that we modeled after Bill Martin's <u>Brown Bear</u>. The children are really enjoying this book as they love to look at the pictures of themselves and their new friends. This book is one, of many activities, that is helping our class become a community of learners. Seeing our names in print and reading them aloud.helps us to remember to use names when speaking to friends thus, helping us all feel more connected and appreciated. Hearing the children read our book together gives us all a warm and welcoming feeling. We are really coming together as a class.

We have been doing a lot of painting these past few days as we have opened our painting easel for children to use at exploration time. With the help of a beautiful story by Cynthia Rylant with pictures by Peter Catalanotto called, <u>All I See,</u> we have been discussing the idea that paintings tell stories. We have encouraged all children to take a turn painting and many beautiful pieces now decorate our classroom.

Our work with shapes continues and we have been traveling around our room on a "shapes safari". The children have been encouraged to look for objects in our classroom that are shaped like a circle, square, or triangle. They are bringing home today a *"Shapes All around Us"* folder that also includes a blank rectangle, oval and diamond in case they would like to hunt for these at home. Other shape activities have included making mosaic pictures out of precut pieces of colored paper. These projects are now on display in our classroom as well.

As a part of all our projects we continue to focus on taking pride in our work and developing fine motor skills. Coloring, printing, and cutting are all skills that young hands need practice to develop. Any help at home with this is appreciated.

Your child may have mentioned that he/she has been asked to meet with me "privately" for an interview. At various times in the year I will be doing this so that I can assess the progress that he/she is making in some of our skill areas. We will discuss my findings during conference times. I try to make this like a game for children and they seem to enjoy having this one on one time with me. This is not to be stressful in any way but rather, another opportunity for me to get to know your child as a learner.

During "reading together" time this week we introduced a story and a song that both contain lots of rhymes. *Down By the Bay* has quickly become a song that children are asking to sing over and over. The book, <u>did you ever see?</u> by Walter Einsel made us all laugh as we tried to predict the silly rhymes in the text. We will continue to listen for rhyming words as well as make rhymes on our own in the coming weeks. Having children play with language like this and also listen for the sounds that are necessary for making a rhyme is an important and fun aspect of our language and literacy program.

We have been busy. A quick reminder, NO SCHOOL tomorrow, or Monday. Have a great weekend.

ル、 *Becky*

the comparison, or to create a business plan for a new school store and submit it to a loan officer. Parents with these or similar occupations could provide feedback on whether or not the students have communicated effectively to their intended audience.

The parent-teacher conference is the most common time for parents and teachers to talk. It is then that you have the greatest opportunity to help parents understand the assessment processes you are using in your classroom. You will want to show the parents your record-keeping systems, so that they recognize how much data you actually collect about each child. However, you cannot expect parents to interpret all these data; they are much too comprehensive. Most parents appreciate your making important generalizations about their children—"Sara has an excellent ability to organize and interpret data," followed by specific examples of evidence of this ability. As noted in Chapter 7, you

FIGURE 9–3. *Becky's October 16 Newsletter*

Room 110 News   October 16, 1992

Dear Parents:

Even with a shortened week we are accomplishing a lot in Kindergarten!

This week we:

* continued working on two rhyming activities. Your child is bringing home one piece of work that he/she has been working on in conjunction with the book, <u>did you ever see?</u> by Walter Einsel
* estimated how many apples were in a bag.
* conducted an apple taste test using red delicious, granny smith, McIntosh and yellow/golden delicious apples. I must admit the children had a lot of fun with this activity. We collected data about our taste test and then recorded the data on a graph that is on display in our classroom.
* estimated how many seeds were inside one McIntosh apple.
    Before we counted the actual number of seeds in this apple, I told the children a story about the little red house with no windows and no doors, a little brown chimney and a star inside. Many were amazed when I took out our apple and cut it open, lying on its side, to find that there is a star inside. They have asked, "Do all apples have stars inside?" When we counted the seeds in this apple and found that there were 10, they asked, "Do all apples have ten seeds?" Needless to say we will be investigating these questions further. Any research or data collection you can do at home would be appreciated.
* listened to a wonderful storyteller, Valerie Tutson, provided for us by the PTA.

All in all it's been a fast and exciting four days!

For Our Art Center, We're Looking For:

    toilet paper/paper towel tubes
    buttons
    fabric swatches
    meat trays
    and any other interesting items you'd like to donate to the cause.

                                        Thanks!!   *Becky*

P. S. Many children have asked for the words to *Down By the Bay*, so here they are. Happy singing! Happy Rhyming!

FIGURE 9–4.　*Parent Questionnaire*

My Child

Child's Name:

Parent(s):

You know your child so well. Please take a few minutes to help me learn from you.

What toys does your child like best?

_____

_____

What interests does your child have?

_____

_____

What types of books does your child enjoy?

_____

_____

What things does your child count or sort at home?

_____

_____

What else would you like me to know about your child?

_____

_____

_____

FIGURE 9–5.　*Interview Guide*

When you finish your assignment, meet with a parent or an adult. Tell the parent or adult your answers to these questions. Ask him or her to record your answers.

How did you record the times that family members spent reading?

How did you figure out the total amount of time that family members spent reading?

How did you display your data clearly?

What is an example of something that you learned from your data?

The name of the adult I met with is _____.

might also consider a parent-*child*-teacher conference in which the child shares her portfolio with her parents. The parent-teacher conference is also a time to reinforce the content and performance standards on which you are focusing, helping parents identify and recognize the mathematical abilities you value and thus assess.

Many teachers find they have more successful parent conferences after they have adopted alternative assessment techniques. Teachers report being clearer about their goals and their standards of performance, and they have more anecdotal data about each child's relationship to those standards. Parents report greater satisfaction when conferences help them better understand the goals of the classroom and where their children stand in relation to those goals. Most children also prefer to be evaluated in terms of a developing ability rather than in comparison to one another.

If parents are able to visit your classroom, help supervise a field trip, or participate in a classroom mathematical investigation, they will observe your assessment strategies in action. They will see you interview a child, take notes, and arrange peer assessments. They can also be of invaluable help in accomplishing these tasks. Back-to-school nights are another vehicle for explaining your program. You may even want to arrange a special Family Math Night, during which families explore mathematical games and activities together. For parents who are unable to visit the school, you may want to videotape an important presentation or performance and send it home.

Many towns and school districts have established math committees in the past few years and given them the responsibility for steering the system through this reform movement. They may collect resources, choose new textbooks, create curriculum guides, develop open-ended problems and scoring rubrics, and bring in consultants to conduct professional development sessions. Committees like this make it possible for a few parents to become very involved and knowledgeable about the reform and how their school system is implementing changes. These parents can be a valuable resource in helping you find ways to communicate with other parents.

Although they don't occur every week, over time the notes, calls, newsletters, surveys, assignments, conferences, evening events, classroom visits, and committee work give rich opportunities to include parents in the learning and assessment activities of your classroom.

What do I do about report cards?

The report card is often still viewed as the most significant reporting mechanism. Although the new assessment strategies focus on ways to gain evidence of learning that allow you to provide a rich description of each child's development in relationship to specific standards, many of you may teach in school systems that require grades to be given on report cards. While this may be less true at the primary level, primary students nonetheless develop an interest in grades because their older siblings in upper elementary or middle school receive them and discuss them with their parents.

Most of us can still remember a grade we got in a college course or paper. It is much less likely that we can remember a particular descriptive comment. The grade serves as a summative statement of the performance. It is the expected answer to the question, How did you do? Further, grades are seen as more objective than descriptive writings, particularly in a mathematics classroom. If you think back on your own mathematics courses, you can probably remember nightly homework that was graded according to the percentage of questions you answered correctly. Quizzes and tests were graded the same way. The average of those scores then became your grade. Since anyone could take those same scores and arrive at the same grade, this is often viewed as an objective process. However, many subjective decisions had been made before those scores were determined. Subjective answers had been given to questions like: Will partial credit be given? Which exercises will be assigned for homework? What format should be used for testing? All grading is subjective in one way or another. What is important is making the subjective criteria clear and available.

You may already have descriptive report cards. If you do, you will need to examine all your records of observations and other recording or scoring forms in order to form the important generalizations you wish to communicate. Your previously identified curriculum goals are the areas in which you will make your generalizations. The report card process is therefore very similar to preparing for the parent-teacher conference, although your actual reporting will be more succinct.

Some of you, however, teach in school systems that require a grade or other rating system or a combination of grades, ratings, and comments. You may want to give grades in the same way you use a scoring rubric to score a particular piece of student work. What does an A mean to you? Can you describe the behaviors that you would expect from an A student? As with most complicated issues, you will find it helpful to discuss grading with your peers. Perhaps you can identify a general scoring rubric that can be used to describe performance indicators associated with letter grades. For example, you might expect an A student to have superior reasoning and communication skills, go beyond expected requirements of assignments, effectively apply mathematical understanding to solve real-world problems, and formulate interesting questions and problems that involve mathematics.

Some teachers are more comfortable creating a list of the components (e.g., projects, portfolios, quizzes, homework, and problem sets) they will include in the grading process and allocating a portion of the grade to each element. Over time, teachers may adjust that allocation. For example, a teacher who uses portfolios for the first time may allocate a smaller percentage to portfolios than he will after using portfolios successfully for a few years.

As with all changes, you will need to experiment until you find a technique that works for you. What is most important is that you find a way to include the new assessment strategies you are using in your classroom in your reporting process. You want to validate your work and your students' work in alternative assessment, not treat it as "other." If your district's report card only reports grades, you may want to include a descriptive piece of your own and send it home along with the report card. The piece may include samples of work with the listed criteria, a description of the student's work habits and group work, a list of the student's strengths, and suggestions for ways parents can participate in their child's learning.

You may also want to find out about other school districts' report cards.

Perhaps you and your colleagues could help your school move toward a reporting system that gives more credibility to descriptive reports that provide a depth and breadth of evidence from multiple sources. As parents recognize from your other reporting mechanisms that learning can be reported in a variety of ways, not just through letters or numbers, they may be more supportive of changes in report cards. In fact, many parent-teacher committees in schools are relying on new assessment practices to help them restructure their schools' report cards so that they will be better linked to curricular goals and more developmentally appropriate.

How do assessment strategies effect accountability?

Accountability and public support
Accountability in education continues to play an important role in how we assess and report learning in the classroom. It probably always will. Public money is used to support the educational system, and the public has the right to know that its money is being well spent. Currently, allocation decisions are often based on a comparison of one group of students with another on a district, state, or national level. Most school districts continue to administer standardized tests to compare students' performances.

Standardized tests are designed to rank students with respect to a particular trait or ability. The test administrators assume a population with a normal distribution curve and award test scores accordingly. The tests are used to identify where within the population a particular student falls or to compare aggregated data, such as the mean scores from one community with those from another. The results of these tests often have a powerful political impact when aggregated. They may be used to determine fund allocations, the level of a community's respect for its school system, property values, administrative contracts, and student placement. Therefore, test results receive a great deal of attention and the testing process is often referred to as high-stakes testing. The only indication of student accomplishment available to community members who don't have children in the school system may be these public reports of standardized test results.

Happily, new forms of standardized tests are being developed. In the next few years, many more will be available. As we mentioned in Chapter 1, many states are now using or developing standardized tests that include open-ended questions. Other states and test development centers are pursuing criterion-referenced tests with clearly stated goals. Tests like these fulfill the purposes of standardized testing while also meeting some of the goals of the current assessment agenda. However, education professionals are currently debating whether or not it is possible to meet both of these goals at once. Concerns over the reliability and validity of new forms of standardized tests raise questions about their use and/or whether or not our understanding of the concepts of reliability and validity needs to be expanded.

Some educators question whether we need standardized tests to demonstrate accountability. Grant Wiggins, for example, suggests that "accountability exists when the service provider is obliged to respond to criticism from those whom the provider serves" (1993, p. 257). Wiggins uses the analogy of consumers and manufacturers to demonstrate his point. If consumers are not satisfied with a product, they will stop buying it and switch to one made by another manufacturer. *Consumer Reports* may provide comparative data that hasten the switch, but Wiggins argues that ultimately it is consumer dissatisfaction that keeps the manufacturer accountable, not the test data. Schools will never be fully accountable until they rely not on tests but on ways to be more responsive to their clients. In this model it is the individual teachers and administrators who would be held accountable, not the districts. Data would be collected from students, parents, teachers at the next grade level, and former students, among others. Test (as well as other) data would emphasize comparisons of individual students or schools with themselves over time, in order to determine the *value added*, the level of improvement. Under a model of assessment like this, everyone would be motivated to improve.

Accountability and teacher evaluation

Concern about accountability also impacts teacher evaluation. What makes a good teacher? remains an often-asked question. New criteria for certification have been developed in many states, the notion of tenure has been challenged, and national teaching standards have been suggested. Identifying attributes of good teaching is not unlike identifying what it means to know mathematics. Nearly everyone would include the ability to assess students' knowledge as an important professional standard for teachers. In its *Professional Standards* (1991), the National Council of Teachers of Mathematics has identified performance standards for this professional expectation, including that the teacher

> Uses a variety of assessment methods to determine students' understanding of mathematics.
> Matches assessment methods with the developmental level, the mathematical maturity, and the cultural background of the student.
> Aligns assessment methods with what is taught and how it is taught.
> (p. 110)

As benchmarks for these performance standards are agreed on and made public within your school system or state, the assessment data that you collect in your classroom together with your recording systems could be used as evidence that you have met these performance criteria. In this model of teacher evaluation, the strategies that you use daily in your classroom mirror the strategies used to evaluate your work. The goals of the National Board for Professional Teaching Standards, established in 1987, are to develop rigorous standards for accomplished teachers and to assess teachers wishing to receive National Board Certification in relation to those standards. As one of the Board's assessment tasks, teachers create portfolios in which they collect evidence, over time, to demonstrate that they meet the teaching standards.

How do assessment strategies figure in program evaluations?

Occasionally, a school system is evaluated externally. The evaluation may be called for by the school board, required by an accreditation agency, or mandated statewide. There are many aspects to such an evaluation process. Classes may be observed; teachers, parents, students, and administrators may be interviewed;

and self-study reports may be read. More and more, student products are also part of program evaluations.

Unlike standardized tests, samples of student work can illustrate a student's development over time. They can be used to help define the curricular and instructional goals of your classroom and your standards for meeting those goals. By including student work, you can show how your goals are being met, not merely ask your students to meet the goals of the program standards or evaluator. This is not to say that using external standards or evaluators is negative. It is not. However, external standards should be used in cooperation with internal goals and procedures and should continue to support the teacher's role as the primary assessor of student work.

When school systems lack the internal leadership to develop and use new alternative assessment strategies, an external evaluation can be a very powerful impetus. It provides an additional voice emphasizing how important it is for students to develop mathematical power and for teachers and schools to develop assessment tasks that address that power. States that have initiated standardized tests including open-ended problems have found that these tests have had a profound impact on curriculum and staff development resources. Results of the tests are reported publicly and low scores need to be explained. School districts with low scores are pressured to develop curriculum that will prepare the students to deal with these questions more successfully.

Ideally, external and internal assessments work hand in hand to further the current agenda in mathematics education. Through consistent efforts, they can strengthen classroom practice, empower teachers, and enlighten the public.

How do new reporting systems relate to my teaching?

It is important that your new assessment strategies become incorporated into your school's reporting system. Making them a part of the official system is a way of valuing them, just as excluding them is a way of devaluing them. Reporting your assessment data ensures that your new assessment strategies are recognized.

Reporting your assessment data allows you to communicate with parents, administrators, and state officials in new ways, deemphasizing comparisons among students and focusing on standards that are valued. By talking with parents about the changes you are making in your classroom, you are increasing the likelihood that they will support your efforts. You can provide administrators and officials with specific examples of your students' work and specific examples of your assessment documentation and recording systems. These examples promote more informative and meaningful communication than generalities do. There is no better way to communicate the success of your classroom than through examples of student work, work that provides evidence of mathematical reasoning, applying mathematics to real-world problems, and communication.

More and more schools are relying on outside funding. It is much more likely that you will receive support for your work if it is understood. Your reporting systems can provide a voice for your work and the work of your students that will help you get the support and encouragement you need. It is an essential element in the assessment journey, providing continuous feedback that informs the identification of goals, learning tasks, performance indicators, assessment tasks, and documentation systems.

· 10 ·

Finding the Way:
Three Journeys

*What do you say to teachers about
getting started with assessment? How
have other teachers started?*

Many teachers want to bring alternative assessments into their mathematics classroom, but they are not sure how to go about it. Their reasons for wanting to incorporate assessment into instruction vary. Some teachers have received a district or school mandate to do so. Others have attended an inservice on alternative assessment or the NCTM standards that made them think about what they are currently doing in their classrooms. Still others have benefited from the influence of teaching colleagues who have begun to make some changes in their mathematics lessons and who thus provide permission and support to try out new ideas.

Just as everyone changes for different reasons and to different degrees, individual "journeys through change" in the mathematics classroom look different as well. Some teachers have their goals clearly in place and find themselves in schools or districts that have the resources to support them in reaching those goals. Perhaps the more common journey, though, is less definite, a process of starting and stopping, with some incremental gains each time. For most of us the path through change is not a smooth one. There are conflicts along the way, choices that have to be made, supports for which we are grateful, and impediments that we wish would go away.

This chapter follows three teachers as they incorporate alternative assessment into their mathematics classrooms. These are teachers we have known and who have generously allowed us to use their stories. We want to share the questions they asked, the markers and milestones they passed, the obstacles and support they encountered, and the vision of assessment each holds.

Lorraine

The Journey

Lorraine is completing her master's program at a small liberal arts college in the Northeast. Three years ago a colleague asked whether Lorraine wanted to attend a five-day summer workshop on how to teach mathematics using manipulatives. At the time, Lorraine was teaching fourth grade in a medium-sized suburban school district; she had been an elementary teacher for twelve years.

Lorraine initially agreed to attend the workshop as a favor to her friend, but as the time grew nearer she became excited about it. She had always been uncomfortable as a teacher of mathematics, feeling that she could not do a competent job with her students because she lacked content knowledge. So she looked forward to the workshop as something that might bolster her confidence. She was not disappointed. At the end of those five days, Lorraine felt that for the first time in all the years she had been teaching she had found a way to present mathematics to her students that made sense to her and that she actually enjoyed! She could hardly wait for school to start.

The workshop also introduced her to the NCTM standards. Up until then, Lorraine hadn't heard about the standards and knew nothing about the ideas associated with reform in mathematics. While she was interested in the standards, Lorraine did not see how they would influence her day-to-day teaching. She was, however, eager to try out the ideas she had gathered from the activities at the workshop. Through the workshop activities, Lorraine came to understand mathematics in ways she had not anticipated. Understanding mathematics content better gave her a new confidence as a teacher as well as a sense of energy about teaching mathematics.

When school started that fall Lorraine began to implement many of these ideas. To her delight she found her students were very responsive and had a lot more enthusiasm for mathematics than she remembered encountering in past years. Lorraine concentrated on activities related to estimation, patterns, measurement, and geometric shapes that involved materials she could bring into her class. She even found some manipulatives in a general supply room at her school. As the year progressed, she approached her principal about purchasing some more. The principal was agreeable, allocated a dollar amount, and let Lorraine make the final purchasing decisions.

Throughout the early part of the fall, Lorraine shared her successes with one of the other five fourth-grade teachers. This teacher, Carol, was interested in how Lorraine was changing her mathematics lessons. Carol's husband, a school principal in another town, had spoken about the standards and the changes going on in mathematics education. Over time, Lorraine and Carol became more and more focused on mathematics. Together they attended a couple of regional mathematics workshops that built on Lorraine's summer experiences. In addition, Lorraine attended monthly follow-up meetings to her original workshop.

Lorraine and Carol began to combine their students for mathematics lessons and found this new format to be very successful, both for the students and for them. Their school building had originally been constructed according to the precepts of an open education system, with all the fourth grades occupying one large space. Currently, however, individual class spaces were partitioned off by dividers. Moving students back and forth was therefore comparatively easy, and the students enjoyed the opportunity to work together. By December, Lorraine and Carol knew they were an excellent support system for each other, and they began to talk about regular team teaching. In May they asked the superintendent if they could remove some of the partitions to allow them to share classroom space during the next school year. The superintendent was happy to take the request to the school committee, where it was approved. That summer Lorraine and Carol spent time preparing for the fall.

During the fall, however, problems developed between Lorraine and Carol and the other fourth-grade teachers. Lorraine and Carol felt these teachers were threatened by the changes being introduced, especially the way in which the parents of Lorraine and Carol's students were getting involved in the mathematics curriculum.

Late in September Lorraine and Carol held a parents' information session at which they explained their new approach to mathematics teaching. At this session, they also described how they would be introducing journals into mathematics classes. They hoped the journals would make their students reflect more about their learning as well as give them the opportunity to discuss the "evidence of learning" concept, to grapple with how we know when we have learned something.

The other fourth-grade teachers, seeing ideas that did not fit the traditional way of doing things, began to say and do things meant to isolate Lorraine and Carol from the rest of the staff.

Lorraine and Carol continued to make wonderful progress with student journals. They also introduced elements of a portfolio program. The focus of their students' portfolio work was building and communicating patterns. They found that portfolio assessment gave them information about their students' developing mathematics abilities they didn't always discover through traditional tests. They also noticed that their students seemed to develop a genuine commitment to the portfolios, working with a sense of purpose that Carol and Lorraine had not experienced before.

As wonderful as the in-class progress was, the strain of being set apart from the staff took its toll on Lorraine. By May she had decided not to return. Carol stayed and returned to her own classroom.

In the fall Lorraine enrolled in a full-time master's program. She wanted to understand the process of change in teachers more fully. She believed that, yes, change is hard but that schools need to provide more support for teachers who want to change their practice. She wanted to find out what those supports should be and how they could be integrated into a school structure.

Graduate school has also given Lorraine a chance to learn more about mathematical content and alternative assessment. As part of her master's program she designed a mentor-teacher program she believed would help support teachers through change. Currently, Lorraine is working to implement this mentor-teacher program in a local school district as part of its long-range professional development program for elementary teachers.

Lorraine feels strongly that the professional education community and parents need to realize that change among teachers should happen gradually, since letting go of old ways of doing things and being successful at new approaches can be difficult. Because change takes time, other teachers need to be understanding and supportive. Although she left the classroom, Lorraine still feels very much a part of the professional education community. She is active in local and regional mathematics organizations and is participating in a research project on alternative assessment in mathematics. At this point she is not sure how returning to the classroom fits in with her study of change and assessment. For now her interest lies in helping teachers who are in the classroom understand the pivotal role alternative assessment has in teaching and the dynamics involved in changing one's professional practice to incorporate alternative assessment.

Reflections

Lorraine was motivated to change by a professional development seminar that presented mathematics in a way she found accessible as a learner and could transfer to her classroom. Newly energized, she shared her confidence in mathematics with a colleague who, like Lorraine, was open to changing her mathematics teaching.

Lorraine's growing confidence in mathematics content coupled with her increasing familiarity with the NCTM standards introduced her to new assessment strategies—journals and portfolios. In retrospect, it appears that Lorraine's interest in alternative assessment came from a growing confidence in her mathematical knowledge, while the key to moving the process of change forward was the support she found from another teacher in her building.

At the same time, the resistance she encountered from other teachers in her building was a significant impediment. Being negatively set apart from her colleagues was painful. She experienced a great deal of loneliness and a sense that she was too different.

In an effort to understand change better, Lorraine left the classroom and enrolled in a graduate program that supported her interest in both change and assessment, and it is there that her journey through change and her growth in alternative assessment continues.

Gretchen

The journey

Gretchen is a third-grade teacher in an inner-city school in a large midwestern city. She has taught elementary school for sixteen years, earning a reputation as a skilled teacher of language arts. When the whole language movement emerged in the 1980s, Gretchen was an early proponent. Initially, two aspects of the whole language philosophy caught Gretchen's attention: the emphasis it gave to learning as a process and the central place it gave to the child.

Gretchen's first teaching assignment was fifth grade. She remembers being amazed at how these students struggled with writing, both structure and ideas. Because the students were so intimidated by the process, it was very difficult to get them to do any kind of creative writing. Gretchen enjoyed writing herself and couldn't understand why her students didn't. But given a new teacher's struggle to prepare for each new day, this concern faded into the background.

In her seventh year of teaching, Gretchen began to read some articles about process writing and immediately identified what had been troubling her about her students' fear of writing. Writing had not been treated like a process; students were not allowed to work through the process of drafts and revisions to a finished product as real writers do. Of course! The pedagogy she had used with her students assumed that they were ready to present finished drafts for each assignment, that by knowing the rules of grammar and the technical signals of writing they would be able to produce a good final product.

After reading several more articles on process writing, Gretchen asked the district curriculum specialist in language arts whether he knew of other process writing materials. He referred her to a faculty member in the School of Education at the local university, Dr. Simpson, who had written some articles about process writing. Gretchen called her and was invited to attend a two-day workshop on process writing Dr. Simpson was giving at the end of the month. This workshop was a turning point in Gretchen's teaching career. She met other teachers who were asking some of the same questions she was about how to build self-confidence in and a positive disposition toward writing. This workshop asked participants to reflect on some questions about learning in general: How can we come to see students as individuals with developing skills that may not conform to theoretical benchmarks of growth? As teachers, how do we recognize when learning is taking place? What are the essential skills of a good writer? These questions stayed with Gretchen as she began to implement a process writing program in her fifth-grade class. Along the way she attended other workshops on process writing and talked frequently with teachers she met at these workshops.

Gretchen enjoyed theorizing with her colleagues, but her greatest joy was the change she saw in her students' attitude toward writing and in the quality of what they wrote. The component of her program she felt best about was a writers conference in which students not only displayed their work but also discussed the writing process among themselves and with their parents. Listening to her students describe the draft and revision process, Gretchen felt closest to finding answers to some of the questions posed at her first workshop. She caught glimpses of individual students' learning, the motivation and direction behind the revision process.

What her process writing program did not do was make grading easier. She found it extremely difficult to assign a letter grade to the writing assignments. The grade seemed to take away the richness of the student's journey through the writing process. At the same time she felt trapped, since her principal and the parents of her students depended on grades as a form of accountability of work done in the classroom.

In 1989, Gretchen was asked to be a third-grade teacher in a specialty school in mathematics and science. It was a difficult decision. She had been teaching fifth grade for almost eleven years; she was comfortable with what she was doing and comfortable with her colleagues. Most important, she believed she was a good teacher at this grade level. But in the end, she decided to join the staff of the magnet school.

During her initial inservice session at her new school the following August, she was introduced to the NCTM's *Curriculum and Evaluation Standards for School Mathematics*. It was clear that the district hoped this specialty school would build these goals into each classroom. When she listened to the district mathematics specialist describe these instructional goals and talked about them with the other third-grade teachers, she was struck by their similarity to the goals of process writing. Both focused on involving students in learning as a process in which there are opportunities for reflection and revision and which means more than memorizing rules and definitions. Both also emphasized building self-confidence in traditionally difficult subjects. Gretchen listened to her new colleagues' descriptions of their own struggles with traditional forms of testing and grading, which seemed to them to work against the idea of learning as a process and the importance of self-confidence.

Even though Gretchen felt her background in mathematics and science was not as strong as that of her colleagues, she knew her experience with process writing would be of real value in implementing the standards in their third-grade classrooms. Gretchen became a building leader, supporting teachers who wanted to introduce a more process-oriented form of instruction into their classroom and who wanted to use portfolios as part of their evaluation of student work.

Discussions about portfolios gave these teachers an opportunity to discuss student evaluation in general. Often these discussions focused on the question that had caught Gretchen's attention at her first workshop on process writing: How can we tell when a student has learned something? There was clear agreement among most of the teachers in Gretchen's new school that standardized tests do not provide evidence of learning. They realized that not all students do well on tests and that questions emphasizing one correct solution do not tell teachers what students are understanding or not understanding.

With the help of district funds, the kindergarten through fifth-grade teachers at Gretchen's school explored using more open-ended mathematics problems as a way to link assessment and instruction. Drawing from a variety of resources, the teachers were free to create open-ended problems they felt would give them the kinds of information they thought were important about how their students understood mathematics.

Gretchen was an active and committed participant in the exploration of how to link instruction and assessment. She brought to the discussions her experiences with process writing and her general interest in questions about learning. With the help of her colleagues and the guidance of documents like the NCTM's *Curriculum and Evaluation Standards for School Mathematics*, she was able to return to questions she had struggled with as a beginning teacher. She believes the discussions about alternative assessment were the link that had been missing throughout her entire teaching career, revealing a way in which evaluation could serve a positive role in informing a teacher about learning.

Reflections

A teacher's having previously been involved in process writing often makes it easier for her to change her mathematics teaching in ways that incorporate a process approach. This was certainly Gretchen's experience. Gretchen did not have a great deal of confidence in her knowledge of mathematics content, but she had some very successful experiences with her students and with colleagues in introducing a process approach into language arts instruction. Because of her previous successes and experiences, she was able to see connections between a process approach in language arts and mathematics.

Gretchen's journey has been gradual and ongoing. Her work in process writing started early in her teaching career; little by little she found the opportunities, the colleagues, and the resources to change her approach to teaching language arts. Thus, the decision to push herself professionally, to focus on mathematics, was perhaps not as difficult as it might have been. Along the way she had the good fortune to find other teachers with whom she could network, as well as university connections that served as an ongoing resource. Moving into an environment structured to support teachers in incorporating the NCTM standards into their classroom was important. It was also important that administrators allowed these teachers to question past evaluation practices and supported them by giving them the time and resources they needed. Gretchen will push further into her investigation of student assessment. Right now she believes she is beginning to understand the power of alternative assessment to unify instruction.

Mason

The journey

Mason is a sixth-grade teacher in the rural school district he attended as a child. He graduated from the local state university and has taught for five years. During these years he has been most challenged and perplexed by one issue: standardized testing. When his principal asked him to serve on a districtwide task force that would ultimately develop a position paper on the role of standardized testing in the district, he eagerly accepted the opportunity to debate and discuss the topic.

Mason generally has a class of about twenty-eight students, with a range of attitudes toward school in general and mathematics in particular. Some are enthusiastic; others lack self-confidence and interest. At the same time, Mason has noticed a similarity in their learning styles. Having grown up in an area where children start to work alongside family members on the family farm at an early age, most of these students learn best in hands-on situations. Mason recalls times from his own childhood when he and his brother and sister were given tasks they had to figure out how to do on their own, either by trial and error or by watching others. Working alongside others as a child, he made adjustments based on the feedback he received. These early habits of learning carried over into adulthood and his teaching philosophy.

Mason knows that mathematics can be a hard subject for children, not because the concepts are difficult but because it is often taught apart from real-life contexts and applications. Whenever possible, then, Mason tries to create mathematics lessons that place students in an active, investigative role: collecting, organizing, and representing data; interpreting and finding patterns and relationships in real data (charts depicting monthly rainfall or temperatures, for example); and discovering the connections among number operations through a variety of problem-solving scenarios. Observing students in the process of learning is important to him, not just the answers they obtain. Through his observations, Mason sees the choices students make as they work toward solutions. In turn, those choices provide Mason with good insight into a student's understanding of mathematical concepts.

Mason's philosophy of teaching was influenced by his student teaching experiences as well. When Mason was a student teacher in a seventh-grade class, his cooperating teacher offered excellent examples of how to structure open-ended lessons. This teacher had a profound effect on Mason's sense of what classrooms should look like when children are engaged in the learning process. Mason had not expected any excitement for mathematics—he certainly did not have it as a student—and was surprised by the enthusiasm of these seventh graders.

In one series of mathematics lessons presented in Mason's student teaching classroom, the students were investigating the relationships among measurement, geometry, ratios, and percents by designing and building their own houses out of cardboard. As he observed the children working in pairs he was impressed by their ability to talk about the mathematics they applied in making decisions about designing and building. For example, the students were free to design whatever kind of floor plan they wanted within the confines of a square-foot limitation. Students discussed the pros and cons of certain designs, using data on room dimensions and percentages of functional living space.

During his first years of teaching Mason felt somewhat successful at creating a classroom in which project-based instruction was the focus, particularly in mathematics. A greater problem was what he considered the mismatch between his open-ended instructional style and the school's expectation that student achievement would be measured through very traditional forms of testing. At least twice each year, Mason was pressured by his principal to prepare his students for state and national mathematics tests. Inexperienced as he was, Mason nevertheless believed that standardized tests often failed to tap all the knowledge students had about a subject like mathematics. Tests focusing on memorized facts and procedures did not reveal many of the skills Mason was teaching in his classroom. He felt, for example, that standardized tests never captured a student's ability to set up a problem based on raw information. These tests had already configured the information into a standardized format; the student's job was to compute the correct answer. And Mason found that when he did try to prepare his students for these tests he had to change his whole instructional approach, which confused them. He felt he was sending his students mixed messages. He generally had his students work in groups, encouraging collaboration. Two weeks before the series of standardized tests he had his students put their desks back into rows and told them they had to do their work alone.

Mason tried to talk with his colleagues about this mismatch between his philosophy of teaching and learning and standardized tests. He found most to be unsympathetic; they told him he was creating his own problem by teaching in a style that did not prepare students for mandated testing. He compared his students' test results with other students at the same grade level and found his students generally scored quite well in the problem-solving portion but were less successful in portions involving the greatest time pressure, particularly computation. Since he believed mathematics was a great deal more than computation, he tended not to worry if his students' scores were not as high in this area. At the same time, he knew poor scores would get students tracked into lower-level mathematics classes.

Because administrators in Mason's district expected students to score well in number facts and computation, Mason felt caught in the middle. He wanted to be viewed as a successful teacher and he felt that the prevailing opinion was that successful teaching resulted in high test scores.

In his role as a member of the district's standardized testing task force, Mason went to a three-day district workshop on alternative assessment, a new term for him. The workshop was valuable for two reasons. He was surrounded by teachers who were asking some of the same questions he had been asking, and he began to understand something he had intuitively felt since he started to teach, that student evaluation should be an important part of instruction, not separate and apart from it.

The workshop on alternative assessment prompted Mason to think about how to coordinate inquiry-based instruction with compatible strategies for assessing student work. The idea that assessment should be designed to improve student performance, not just monitor it, made a great deal of sense. He also found support for the idea that student evaluation should be more than a series of scores reported as percentages or letter grades. People talked about how much student work is lost when performance information is reduced to number or letter grades and how students themselves seem perplexed by what number and letter grades mean. Mason finds that students are more concerned with the numbers and letters than with what they say about their individual strengths and weaknesses in a subject.

Mason's favorite part of teaching is the opportunity to observe students in action, applying ideas and information from textbooks, class discussions, discussions among themselves, and experiences outside the classroom. After attending the workshop on alternative assessment, Mason knew that if he could find manageable ways to record these informal observations, the descriptions would help him plan future lessons and have more effective conferences with his students and with their parents. He heard a number of suggestions at the workshop, some of which he plans to implement in the fall.

Mason plans to concentrate his professional development time and resources over the coming year on alternative assessment. His long-term goal is to learn as much as he can about alternative assessment, so that he can talk persuasively with his principal and other administrators about the importance of looking at different student evaluation strategies. Along the way, he hopes to share information on assessment with his colleagues. Mason says it's hard to believe a three-day workshop could make such a difference in his professional life. Yet an opportunity to begin to find an answer to the relationship between instruction and assessment validated his educational philosophy; now his journey into alternative assessment begins.

Reflections

Mason's introduction to alternative assessment was prompted by his search to reconcile his philosophy of teaching with traditional methods of evaluation. Looking back on Mason's story, we see an earlier theme emerge as well, that of loneliness and feeling separate from colleagues whose teaching philosophies are very different. Lorraine and Carol also had an ideological conflict that set them apart from their colleagues. For Mason, as for Lorraine, finding colleagues with similar questions and energy for change was key to exploring alternative assessment.

Mason's appointment to the district task force on standardized testing was also an important stimulus for change. It got him to a professional development seminar on alternative assessment. His student teaching experiences and his experiences in learning as a child gave him a vision of how he wanted students to learn, and he could not reconcile standardized testing to that vision. Learning about alternative assessment confirmed his intuitive sense of how important it is to link instruction with assessment. That validation gave him permission to begin to link the two more explicitly in his classroom.

Teachers come to alternative assessment by a variety of pathways. Some are introduced to assessment because of a school or district mandate. Some are working with other teachers to create curriculum frameworks in mathematics. Some take a renewed interest in mathematics after studying the NCTM *Standards*. And others are searching for something that has a better fit with their overall philosophy of education. These multiple paths are important—they reveal a diversity among teachers and within the teaching profession that is not always appreciated. They also affirm the critical role of the teacher in integrating assessment into the mathematics classroom. That said, there is no absolute right way to go about that integration.

Teachers have a pivotal, central place in the overall efforts to reform mathematics in terms of assessment and instruction. Ultimately, teachers are the ones who will define assessment and at the same time make links among curriculum, instruction, and assessment come alive in the classroom. It is therefore critical that along with learning the best way to integrate asessment into the mathematics classroom, we pay equal attention to the road by which teachers come to alternative assessment. The questions they've asked, the conflicts they've experienced, the connections they've made, and the visions they've shaped contribute significantly to our understanding of the role of alternative assessment.

As you continue or begin your own exploration of alternative assessment, we encourage you to share your journey with others. Alternative assessment is emerging as a force that will shape the teaching of every subject in every classroom across this country. It links assessment and instruction in a way very different from how they have traditionally been linked. Attitudes toward student evaluation are also changing. Classrooms are less focused on teaching only what will be tested. A clarity is forming about the importance of teaching as a process of understanding the whole of learning, the whole student, not just the answers the student produces. Assessment plays an important role in expanding our understanding of learning and teaching, and this emerging understanding will be helped enormously when teachers share their "journeys through change."

GLOSSARY

Alternative assessment is just one of the names given to nontraditional methods of evaluating student learning. These different names are often used interchangeably, although each term emphasizes a different aspect of the general concept. Alternative assessment emphasizes that methods used to collect information about student learning are different from traditional paper-and-pencil tests, which are standardized and often appear in a multiple-choice format.

Analytic scoring is a process for assigning a score to a student product. Separate ratings are assigned to different components of the response. The sum of the ratings is the score given to the student's work.

Anchor papers are examples of student work that correspond to a rating scale and can be used as a guide for assigning scores to other examples of student work.

Assessment strategy refers to the way in which information about student learning is collected. Assesment strategies include interviews, observations, portfolios, projects, journals, open-ended questions, and self- and peer assessments.

Authentic assessment is another term used to refer to nontraditional assessment practices. The term emphasizes the fact that assessment tasks must authentically represent the way in which the learning has been conducted, be worthwhile, represent the way in which the tasks would be conducted in the world outside the school, and make sense to students.

Behavioral objectives provide a detailed set of benchmarks, based on grade level, indicating students' mastery of specified procedural skills (addition facts, for example). Traditionally, curriculums were written based on the assumption that a child with average abilities might achieve stated objectives at certain grade levels and periods of time within a grade level.

Clinical interviews were originally used in clinical settings to research students' thinking. In mathematical classrooms they can provide students with opportunities to model and explain their understanding of mathematical concepts. A script, or protocol, is sometimes used to ensure that interviews of all students follow a similar structure.

A **conceptual map** is a graphic representation of the interrelationship of skills and abilities a particular standard of content may comprise. It depicts this interrelationship as a network of related abilities or concepts.

Content standards are specific curricular outcomes that have been identified as essential to mathematical literacy. Each of the thirteen NCTM curriculum and evaluation standards is a content standard.

Convergent thinking involves the ability to select and follow the steps necessary to produce the one correct answer to a problem.

Cooperative learning groups are small groups of students working together. The emphasis in this collaboration is on students communicating their ideas in order to help one another learn.

Cooperative problem solving is a specific example of cooperative learning. This term is sometimes used when the group is focusing on a problem-solving task.

Debriefing is a strategy for guiding students through a self-assessment or peer assessment process. Debriefing is structured around a number of open-ended questions designed to help students think about the learning task just completed.

Descriptive data or **anecdotal data** are narrative rather than numerical documentations of student work. These terms are applied to notes taken while observing a student engaged in a learning task or while reviewing completed student work. The observation or review of student work is done in relation to previously identified assessment criteria and instructional goals that have been shared with the students.

Diagnostic interview is a synonym for clinical interview.

Divergent thinking involves the ability to generate a variety of answers to a problem for which more than one answer may be correct.

A **documentation system** is any tool for organizing anecdotal evidence taken from completed student work or in-class observations that provides an overview of how students are doing on the performance standard or performance indicator being assessed.

Evidence can be thought of as examples obtained from student products or recorded descriptions of student performances that are indicative of student behaviors relative to performance standards and performance indicators.

Formative evaluation is evaluation based on data collected before the instructional unit is completed. When you gather assessment data during a lesson, chapter, or curriculum unit, that data can be used to help develop the remainder of the instructional cycle.

Holistic scoring is a process for assigning a score to a student product in which a single rating is assigned to a student's overall response.

Informal assessment is also used to refer to nontraditional assessment practices. This term emphasizes the informal and ongoing nature of the ways in which data may be collected in contrast to the formality of a written exam. This informality makes it easier for assessment strategies to be incorporated into the instructional process.

Open-ended problems have more than one answer and/or can be solved in a variety of ways. Their "openness" allows a variety of perspectives and can stimulate interest in the communication of mathematical ideas.

Outcomes, such as "organizing and interpreting data," are broad abilities around which curriculum and lessons are developed. These "big ideas" define what is important to be learned and, therefore, assessed.

In **peer assessment,** classmates have an opportunity to reflect on one another's work according to criteria with which they are familiar and which makes sense to them.

Performance assessment is yet another term used to refer to alternative assessment practices. This terms emphasizes the active nature of assessment tasks. For example, we can find out what students know about measuring by observing them perform measurement tasks.

Performance indicators give an idea of what student success looks like in terms of content and performance standards. The descriptions often reflect a continuum of development.

Performance standards are descriptive statements that make clear what a student needs to do in order to provide evidence of having learned a specific content standard. Performance standards help answer a question such as, How do we know a student is a successful problem solver in mathematics?

Portfolio implies a collection of materials that is able to be carried, that can move through time with students. In contrast to traditional measures of student evaluation, portfolios can provide a picture of student performance in mathematics over time.

A **process folio** is a folder in which students keep work that falls under designated portfolio categories. This collection of work provides students with an opportunity to include their best pieces in each category.

Project-based instruction focuses on activities that usually last longer than one lesson and often involve more than one subject. Students may work independently or in small groups, and the project often evolves as student interest is defined.

Protocols define the interview conditions and possible questions. A script may be provided and rules of interaction established so that interview conditions will be similar regardless of the particular interviewer or interviewee.

Rubrics provide a way to organize and interpret the evidence from a student product or student performance. They suggest a continuum of performance levels or indicators associated with the ability or task being assessed.

Scaffolding is a term often used to describe building up a student's mental network of ideas over time. This scaffold or network provides a student with a conceptual understanding of more abstract ideas.

Self-assessment in education means taking the time to understand who and where one is as a learner. When students reflect on their learning experience, noting what happened, what they learned, how it was different from other learning experiences, what was confusing, in what parts of the experience they had the greatest success, they are engaged in self-assessment.

Standards are public statements about what is valued in a curriculum. Standards define locally, statewide, or nationally what will be emphasized in a particular subject without specifying exactly how it will be taught.

Summative evaluation is evaluation that is conducted immediately after the instructional unit is completed. A unit test, a chapter test, and completed projects are examples of this type of evaluation. Summative evaluation is used to measure student learning and, at times, the appropriateness of the instructional techniques and materials.

Validity is an essential component of assessment tasks. The tasks must assess what they purport to assess and reflect the kinds of instructional tasks with which the student is familiar. Inferences that assessors make must be supported through multiple sources of evidence across assessment tasks.

REFERENCES

Ann Arbor Public Schools. 1993. *Alternative Assessment: Evaluating Student Performance in Elementary Mathematics*. Palo Alto, CA: Ann Arbor Public School System.

Artzt, Alice, and Claire Newman. 1990. *How to Use Cooperative Learning in the Mathematics Classroom*. Reston, VA: National Council of Teachers of Mathematics.

Association for Supervision and Curriculum Development. 1989. *Educational Leadership* 46. (Focus issue on assessment.)

———. 1992. *Educational Leadership* 49. (Focus issue on assessment.)

Badger, Elizabeth. 1992. "More than Testing." *Arithmetic Teacher* 39:7–11.

Berlak, Harold, et al. 1991. *Towards a New Science of Educational Testing and Assessment*. Albany, NY: State University of New York.

Blomberg, Fran, et al. 1986. *A Pilot Study of Higher Order Thinking Skills: Assessment Techniques in Science and Mathematics*. Final Report, Parts 1 and 2. Princeton, NJ: National Assessment of Educational Progress.

California Assessment Program. 1989. *A Question of Thinking: A First Look at Students' Performance on Open-Ended Questions in Mathematics*. Sacramento, CA: California State Department of Education.

Carlson, Sybil. 1987. *Creative Classroom Testing*. Princeton, NJ: Educational Testing Service.

Champagne, Audrey, et al. 1991. *Assessment in the Service of Instruction*. Washington, DC: American Association for the Advancement of Science.

Charles, Randall, et al. 1987. *How to Evaluate Progress in Problem Solving*. Reston, VA: National Council of Teachers of Mathematics.

Clarke, David. 1988. *Assessment Alternatives in Mathematics*. Canberra, Australia: Curriculum Corporation.

Corwin, Rebecca, et al. 1990. *Seeing Fractions*. Sacramento, CA: California State Department of Education.

Davidson, Neil, ed. 1990. *Cooperative Learning in Mathematics*. Reading, MA: Addison-Wesley.

Diez, Mary, and Jean Moon. 1990. "Stimulating Thought and Learning in Preschool and Elementary Years." In *Learning to Learn Across the Lifespan*, edited by R. M. Smith. San Francisco: Jossey-Bass.

———. 1992. "What Do We Want Students to Know and Other Important Questions." *Educational Leadership* 49:38–41.

Finn, Chester, Jr. 1991. *We Must Take Charge*. New York: Basic Books.

Greenes, Carole, et al. 1995. *Techniques of Problem Solving: Communication Deck, Grades 1–2*. Palo Alto, CA: Dale Seymour Publications.

Herman, Joan, et al. 1992. *A Practical Guide to Alternative Assessment*. Alexandria, VA: Association for Supervision and Curriculum Development.

Hill, Bonnie, and Cynthia Ruptic. 1994. *Practical Aspects of Authentic Assessment: Putting the Pieces Together*. Norwood, MA: Christopher Gordon.

Kamii, Constance, ed. 1989. *Achievement Testing in the Early Grades: Games People Play*. Washington, DC: National Association for the Education of Young Children. (Address: 1834 Connecticut Ave., NW, Washington, DC 20009.)

Kroll, Diana, et al. 1992a. "Cooperative Problem Solving: But What About Grading?" *Arithmetic Teacher* 39:17–23.

———. 1992b. "Grading Cooperative Problem Solving." *Mathematics Teacher* 85:619–627.

Kulm, Gerald, ed. *Assessing Higher Order Thinking in Mathematics*. Washington, DC: American Association for the Advancement of Science.

Lambdin, Diana, and Vickie Walker. 1994. "Planning for Classroom Portfolio Assessment." *Arithmetic Teacher* 41:318–24.

Leder, Gila, ed. 1992. *Assessment and Learning of Mathematics*. Victoria, Australia: The Australian Council for Educational Research.

Lesh, Richard, and Susan Lamon, eds. 1992. *Assessment of Authentic Performance in School Mathematics*. Washington, DC: American Association for the Advancement of Science.

Long, Madeline, and Neir Ben Hur. 1991. "Informing Learning Through the Clinical Interview." *Arithmetic Teacher* 38:44–46.

Massachusetts Department of Education. 1989. *On Their Own: Student Response to Open-Ended Tests in Mathematics*. Quincy, MA: Massachusetts Department of Education.

Mathematical Sciences Education Board. 1993a. *Measuring Counts: A Policy Brief*. Washington, DC: National Academy Press.

———. 1993b. *Measuring Up: Prototypes for Mathematics Assessment*. Washington, DC: National Academy Press.

Medina, Noe, and Monty Neill. 1990. *The Fallout from the Testing Explosion: How 100 Million Standardized Exams Undermine Equity and Excellence in America's Public Schools*. 3d ed. Cambridge, MA: Fair Test.

Moon, Jean. 1992. "Common Understandings for Complex Reforms." *Education Week* 12 (October 28):23.

National Assessment for Educational Progress. 1987. *Learning by Doing*. Princeton, NJ: Educational Testing Service.

National Commission on Testing and Public Policy. 1990. *From Gatekeeper to Gateway: Transforming Testing in America*. Chestnut Hill, MA: Boston College Center for the Study of Testing, Evaluation, and Public Policy.

National Council of Teachers of Mathematics. 1989. *Curriculum and Evaluation Standards for School Mathematics.* Reston, VA: NCTM.

———. 1991. *Professional Standards for Teaching Mathematics.* Reston, VA: NCTM.

———. 1993. *Assessment Standards for School Mathematics.* Working Draft. Reston, VA: NCTM.

Niss, Mogens, ed. 1993a. *Cases of Assessment in Mathematics Education: An ICMI Study.* Dordrecht, The Netherlands: Kluwer.

———. 1993b. *Investigations into Assessment in Mathematics Education: An ICMI Study.* Dordrecht, The Netherlands: Kluwer.

Pandey, Tej. 1991. *A Sampler of Mathematics Assessment.* Sacramento, CA: California Department of Education.

———. 1993. *Addendum to a Sampler of Mathematics Assessment.* Sacramento, CA: California Department of Education.

Perrone, Vito. 1991. *Expanding Student Assessment.* Alexandria, VA: Association for Supervision and Curriculum Development. (Address: 1250 N. Pitt Street, Alexandria, VA 22314.)

Resnick, Lauren. 1987. *Education and Learning to Think.* Washington, DC: National Resource Council.

Romberg, Thomas, ed. 1992. *Mathematics Assessment and Evaluation: Imperatives for Mathematics Educators.* Albany, NY: SUNY Press.

Sammons, Kay, et al. 1992. "Linking Instruction and Assessment in the Mathematics Classroom." *Arithmetic Teacher* 39:11–16.

Schifter, Deborah, and Catherine Fosnot. 1992. *Reconstructing Mathematics Education: Starting of Teacher Meeting the Challenge of Reform.* New York: Teachers College.

Stenmark, Jean, ed. 1989. *Assessment Alternatives in Mathematics: An Overview of Assessment Techniques that Promote Learning.* Berkeley, CA: EQUALS.

———. 1991. *Mathematics Assessment: Myths, Models, Good Questions, and Practical Suggestions.* Reston, VA: NCTM.

Tierney, Cornelia and Mary Berle Carman. 1995. "Fair Shares" *Investigations in Number, Data and Space.* Palo Alto, CA: Dale Seymour Publications.

Vermont Department of Education. 1991. *Report of Vermont's Mathematics Portfolio Assessment Program.* Montpelier, VT: Vermont Department of Education.

Wiggins, Grant. 1989. "A True Test: Towards More Authentic and Equitable Assessment." *Phi Delta Kappan* 70:703–713.

———. 1992. Creating Tests Worth Taking. *Educational Leadership* 8:26–35.

———. 1993. *Assessing Student Performance: Exploring the Purpose and Limits of Testing.* San Francisco: Jossey-Bass.

Wolf, Dennie, and Nancy Pistone. 1991. *Taking Full Measure: Rethinking Assessment Through the Arts.* New York: The College Board.

DATE DUE

NOV 0 6 2002			

DEMCO 38-297